THE 16 PERSONALITY TYPES

Profiles, Theory, & Type Development

Dr. A.J. Drenth

Published by Inquire Books

ISBN 978-0-9792168-3-1

CONTENTS

INTRODUCTION

We come to personality typology seeking clarity about who we are and how we should live. If the world is a stage, home to innumerable acts and actors, we want to know our role and the story we are living out. Typology helps us understand our natural roles and strengths. It also provides valuable guidance and insight with respect to our careers, relationships, and personal growth.

Historically, most typologies have focused exclusively on *conscious* personality traits, such as being warm, friendly, quirky, analytical, etc. And while understanding our conscious personality is certainly useful and important, it really only gives us half the story. The other half, explored by Freud, Jung, and others, is home to our less conscious or subconscious personality—the beliefs, attitudes, needs, and desires that live beneath our conscious radar. It is only through understanding both halves, our conscious and less conscious personality, that we ascertain a more comprehensive grasp of who we are and how we can grow and develop.

Carl Jung, a pioneer in the field of typology and author of the 1913 classic, *Psychological Types*, always kept at least one eye on the unconscious. For Jung, the conscious personality was really only the tip of the iceberg. In this vein, Jung devoted much time and energy to exploring subconscious symbols and archetypes, as well as what he dubbed the *personal* and *collective unconscious.*

Despite Jung's heroic and trailblazing efforts, he would not have the last word on the unconscious personality. Jung's successors have further illuminated the less conscious personality functions, granting particular attention to the *inferior function*. This can be seen, for instance, in Marie-Louise Von Franz's exploration of the inferior function in *Jung's Typology (1971)*, as well as Naomi Quenk's 1993 book, *Beside Ourselves* (later renamed, *Was That Really Me?*).

For the last decade or so, my colleague Elaine Schallock and I have continued to refine and develop type theory, giving careful consideration to the conscious as well as the less conscious features of the personality types. In *My True Type*, I provide in-depth analyses of each of the personality preferences (E, I, S, N, T, F, J, P) and functions (Ti, Te, Fi, Fe, Si, Se, Ni, Ne), which lay the foundation for this book's personality profiles.

Before diving into the profiles, however, we need to do some preliminary groundwork, some of which is excerpted from *My True Type*. This is to ensure that readers have the necessary tools and background for understanding the underlying theory and language employed in the type profiles.

The Preferences & Functions

According to Myers and Briggs, each personality type has four basic preferences: Introversion (I) or Extraversion (E), Sensing (S) or Intuition (N), Thinking (T) or Feeling (F), and Judging (J) or Perceiving (P).

For example, INFJs prefer I, N, F, and J more than E, S, T, and P. This does not mean that INFJs never utilize E, S, T, or P, but when given the chance, they prefer to use I, N, F, or J.

To illustrate what a personality preference is, I like to compare it to handedness. As we all know, a right-handed person will prefer to use her right hand for the majority of tasks, especially those requiring fine motor skills, such as writing. This of course doesn't mean that she never uses her left hand, but only that it tends to play more of a supportive, rather than a dominant or leading, role.

The same is true for our personality preferences. While we may at times use our non-dominant preferences, in most situations we prefer to lead with our dominant ones. Not only does this feel more comfortable and natural, but typically produces better results.

Of the eight preferences, four of them—Sensing, Intuition, Thinking, and Feeling—also double as functions. Extraversion and Introversion do not qualify as functions because, according to Jung, they primarily represent our preferred *direction of energy and attention*. Extraverts direct their energy and attention *outwardly*, toward people, objects, events, possibilities, etc. Introverts, by contrast, direct their focus *inwardly*, toward themselves—their own thoughts, feelings, intuitions, sensations, etc.

Not only did Jung believe that individuals were characteristically Introverted or Extraverted, but also that each function assumes an introverted or extraverted direction. Thus, when S, N, T, and F are directed inwardly (I) or outwardly (E), we end up with eight functions (Si, Se, Ni, Ne, Ti, Te, Fi, Fe).

But what about Judging and Perceiving? Why aren't they considered functions? The answer is they do play a role in the functions, only less explicitly. Namely, Sensing and Intuition are considered to be Perceiving functions. They are in charge of absorbing, extracting, retaining, or synthesizing information. Thinking and Feeling are Judging functions. Their purpose is to evaluate information and make decisions that contribute to structure, order, and predictability. Hence, the eight functions can be subdivided into Judging and Perceiving functions as follows:

The Judging Functions:

- Introverted Thinking (Ti)
- Extraverted Thinking (Te)
- Introverted Feeling (Fi)
- Extraverted Feeling (Fe)

The Perceiving Functions:

- Introverted Sensing (Si)
- Extraverted Sensing (Se)
- Introverted Intuition (Ni)
- Extraverted Intuition (Ne)

The Functional Stack

Each personality type uses four functions that comprise its functional stack. These functions are ordered according to their relative degree of strength and development, as well as their availability for conscious employment. The most developed and conscious function is called the "dominant function," which is followed by the auxiliary, tertiary, and inferior functions respectively.

The dominant function represents the core strength and defining characteristic of each type. When engrossed in an activity that fully engages the dominant function, we tend to feel alert and alive, doing what we were "born to do." The auxiliary function, which can also be useful and readily developed, might be viewed as the co-pilot or sidekick to the dominant. Falling toward the bottom of the functional stack, the tertiary and inferior are less conscious and less developed than the top two functions. However diminutive their conscious presence, the less conscious functions cannot be ignored. As we will soon discuss, the inferior function, in particular, plays a prominent role in each type's personality dynamics.

Dominant Function: "The Captain;" the signature tool and strength of the personality type

Auxiliary Function: "The Sidekick;" chief assistant to the dominant function

Tertiary Function: "The Adolescent;" relatively unconscious and undeveloped

Inferior Function: "The Child;" the least conscious and developed of the four functions

Here is the INTP's functional stack, which we'll use an example:

Dominant Function: Introverted Thinking (Ti)

Auxiliary Function: Extraverted Intuition (Ne)

Tertiary Function: Introverted Sensing (Si)

Inferior Function: Extraverted Feeling (Fe)

In considering the INTP's functional stack, you may have noticed something curious. Namely, INTPs (and all other types for that matter) use a Thinking, Feeling, Sensing, and Intuiting function. This may be a bit confusing at first, since there is no indication of Sensing (S) or Feeling (F) in their I, N, T, or P preferences. If you look carefully, however, you will notice that their S and F functions are situated *below* their T and N functions. This tells us that INTPs prefer to use T and N (or more specifically Ti and Ne) more than S (i.e., Si) or F (i.e., Fe).

J-P Criteria

Observant readers may have noticed another curious fact about INTPs' functional stack, namely, that despite their status as a P type, their dominant function (Ti) is actually a *Judging* function. The other IP types (i.e., ISTP, INFP, ISFP) also employ a dominant Judging function (Ti or Fi). The situation is reversed for IJs (i.e., INTJ, ISTJ, INFJ, ISFJ), who use a dominant Perceiving function (Ni or Si). This of course makes things more complicated when it comes to understanding IPs and IJs as Judgers versus Perceivers. While this issue is addressed in great depth in *My True Type*, for now, you should work to familiarize yourself with the following J-P criteria:

1. A given type's J-P designation (i.e., the fourth letter of the type) refers largely to its outer (i.e., extraverted) presentation. Hence, J types will extravert a Judging attitude (firm, decisive, opinionated, etc.), while P types will display a Perceiving attitude (open, flexible, receptive, etc.).

2. For Extraverts, the nature of the dominant function (i.e., its status as a Judging or Perceiving function) *matches* their J-P designation. For example, ENTPs' dominant function, Ne, is a Perceiving function and ENTJs' dominant function, Te, is a Judging function.

3. For Introverts, things are more confusing, since the nature of their dominant function *opposes* their J-P designation. We saw this with INTPs above. Namely, despite being classified as a P type, INTPs' dominant function (Ti) is a Judging function. To understand why INTPs and other IPs are considered P rather than J types, refer to number one above.

4. In light of the above, we can make the following associations between the functions and preferences of the various types:

    - Si = SJ types (i.e., Si used as the dominant or auxiliary)
    - Se = SP types
    - Ni = NJ types
    - Ne = NP types
    - Ti = TP types
    - Te = TJ types
    - Fi = FP types
    - Fe = FJ types

The Inferior Function

The inferior function is a less well-known and less-emphasized subject in personality typology. This is not because it is terribly difficult to understand, but because it requires a certain amount of background knowledge about the interplay of the functions in the functional stack.

To a certain extent, each function (i.e., dominant, auxiliary, tertiary, inferior) has its own needs, desires, and agenda. Each wants to have a say in the overall psychic economy. Just as democratic governments strive to integrate the diverse voices of their constituents, each personality type must find ways of integrating the needs and desires of its four functions.

Because the inferior function, sometimes called the lost, missing, or repressed function, is the most unconscious of a type's four functions, it is the most difficult to access and integrate. This is why it is commonly symbolized in dreams as being buried deep underground, undersea, or in a dark forest.

Despite its relative unconsciousness, the inferior function cannot be simply ignored or dismissed as unimportant. To the contrary, it is impossible to achieve psychospiritual wholeness without it! Indeed, the life quest for all types is well viewed as centered on discovering and integrating their "missing function." This quest has been symbolized in religious and literary myths for millennia (e.g., searching for the "promised land" or "Holy Grail"). In his book, *Jung's Four and Some Philosophers*, Thomas King nicely outlines this quest for the elusive inferior function:

> *"The time comes when the individual feels life is empty; something is missing. The original sense of purpose is gone and one is dispirited and confused. At this point the individual feels called to make a difficult search for the rejected (i.e., inferior) function . . . The individual sets out on a difficult and unfamiliar journey (e.g., "a sea voyage," "a venture into the forest") to locate the missing function."*

Here King suggests that we all reach a point in our lives where we suffer what we might call "dominant function fatigue." In other words, we get bored with the humdrum of our dominant function and feel compelled to explore something new and exciting. In King's view, this is a central reason we turn to the inferior function. The inferior engenders a type of experience characteristically distinct from the dominant. Consider the difference, for instance, in seeing and experiencing the world through the lens of logic (T) versus that of the heart (F), or from the point of view of a philosopher (N) versus that of an athlete (S). In light of the stark distinctions, the inferior function is often experienced as magical, mysterious, exciting, or blissful. Some have described it as "a whole new world." It thereby serves as a powerful source of life energy and motivation. This is why all types display a strong appetite for, and curiosity toward, their inferior function.

The "Dark Side" of the Inferior Function

We've seen how the inferior can offer relief from "dominant function fatigue" and serve as a powerful source of energy and motivation for all types. Unfortunately, accessing, much less integrating, the inferior is no small feat. Doing so typically entails a protracted power struggle with the dominant function, one which often entails some measure of pain and suffering. In this respect, the religious myths are correct in suggesting that the road to redemption is often revealed through suffering (e.g., "refinement through fire"). Fortunately, such suffering can be minimized if we can better understand some of the traps and pitfalls of the inferior function.

Because of its relative unconsciousness, the inferior function is responsible for many of our childish, naive, extreme, or delusional thoughts and behaviors. Just as a child fails to realistically apprehend and comprehend the world, so too with the inferior function. For instance, when a typically logical T type imagines love (F) in the manner of a fairy tale, we know he is doing so through the naïve and idealistic lens of his inferior F function.

Despite its ability to distort, exaggerate, or idealize reality, the inferior function is still hard to resist. Because it can be so blissful (e.g., strong feelings of love and infatuation for a thinker), it can easily become a source of addiction. Like all addictions, it may inspire various obsessive, compulsive, or otherwise unhealthy behaviors. When "in the grip" of the inferior function, we may feel locked into certain moods, attitudes, or behaviors that are not easily escaped. We may also become increasingly narrow-minded, irrational, self-indulgent, and irritable. So like any addiction, what begins with a sense of intense pleasure can eventually take a turn for the worse.

In many ways synonymous with the "ego" (in its negative sense), the inferior function is also more sensitive and touchy than the other functions in the functional stack. Individuals who "push our buttons" have usually discovered a way to offend, irritate, or threaten our inferior function. The sort of childish sensitivity and defensiveness associated with the inferior function is closely related to what are commonly described as "ego issues" (e.g., hypersensitivity, ego defensiveness, excessive pride or self-righteousness, etc.).

The inferior function is also a common culprit in type misdiagnoses. For instance, an INFP in the grip of her inferior function (Te) is more apt to mistake herself for a Thinking (e.g., INTP) or Judging type (e.g., INFJ). It is also unfortunate that the confusion caused by the inferior function and other confounding factors has caused many people to prematurely give up on typology or dismiss it as unscientific.

Strategies for Dealing with the Inferior Function

Because it can be experienced as heavenly or hellish, blissful or addictive, all types (especially individuals in Phase II of development) have a love-hate, "can't live with or without it" relationship with their inferior function. In attempting to navigate the complex challenges associated with the inferior, individuals typically employ one or more of the following strategies: avoiding-indulging, crutching, and understanding-integrating.

In working to avoid the darker elements of their inferior function, many people will try a "cold turkey" approach, ignoring or avoiding the desires of the inferior at all costs. Or, they may binge on the inferior for a while and then swing to the opposite extreme of avoiding it. This is the same bipolar, "love-hate" pattern we see in all addictive behaviors.

Another common strategy for dealing with the inferior involves the use of "crutches" that serve to appease or placate it. Examples of crutching include things like persisting in unhealthy relationships (e.g., codependency), clinging to a comforting set of beliefs, or continuing in an unsatisfying job for the sake of financial security.

Such crutches may serve to quell, at least temporarily, inferior-related concerns. The degree to which crutching is viewed as good or bad will largely depend on the individual. More idealistic types may tend to see it as a cop-out, as settling for mediocrity rather than excellence. Others may be more content with crutching, perhaps seeing it as a necessary part of human life.

The last strategy for dealing with the inferior function is working to better understand and integrate it. This involves learning about our type's inferior function and how it has historically manifested in our lives. This may include considering things like:

- How the inferior has influenced our interests and motivations
- The ways in which we have indulged, avoided, or crutched it
- Its relationship to our deepest fears or concerns
- Its role in ego-related behavior, such as hypersensitivity or defensiveness
- Its influence on our ideals and identity, especially our self-ideals
- The ways we've tried to pair or integrate it with our dominant function

In conducting this sort of life analysis, it can be surprising to discover the extent to which the inferior function has influenced our thoughts, behaviors, attitudes, and interests. But by bringing these matters into the light of consciousness, we become more self-aware and less easily swayed by the whims and desires of the inferior function.

Type Development & Integration

Type development involves the development and integration of all the functions in the functional stack, including the inferior function. This of course doesn't happen overnight, but unfolds gradually over the lifespan. The process of type development consists of three general phases.

Phase I: Emergence of the Dominant Function

Extending from early childhood into late adolescence, Phase I of type development is characterized by the emergence and differentiation of the dominant function, along with the relative repression of the other functions. Through this process, the personality becomes divided into conscious and less conscious aspects, with the dominant function serving as the primary seat of conscious awareness and the main tool for navigating life.

Phase II: The Dominant-Inferior Tug-of-War

Once the dominant function reaches a certain threshold of conscious supremacy, the inferior function starts knocking at the door in order to offer us something different. As we saw earlier, the inferior promises a new and intriguing type of experience, one which is characteristically distinct from that of the dominant. As the voice of the inferior gets louder, the inner tension between the dominant and inferior grows stronger.

Once we hear the siren call of the inferior and sample what it has to offer, we cannot help but come back for more. But because the inferior is so unconscious, we often feel forced to leave the dominant function behind in order to seek out or explore the inferior. Doing so can certainly be fun for a while, since, as we've seen, the inferior can engender what amounts to a drug-like high.

But like any drug, the highs of the inferior are fleeting and are almost always followed by lows. Hence, many people begin to tire of constantly looking for their next high. Ultimately, they may conclude that the emotional rollercoaster of indulging the inferior function is not a sustainable or satisfying enterprise.

The challenge then, which is the same for any addict, is finding a viable alternative to the highs of the inferior. We may try to quit the inferior "cold turkey," only to find that life feels dull or arid without it. This leaves us with three basic options, which we discussed earlier, for handling the inferior: indulging-avoiding it, crutching it, or integrating it. Since the latter is central to Phase III, the two mainstays of Phase II are crutching the inferior and alternating between indulging and avoiding it.

One of the most common ways we crutch the inferior is attaching ourselves to an externality that embodies the characteristics of our inferior function. We often do this unwittingly in the type of careers or romantic partner we select. This is why, for instance, we see so many F types pursuing characteristically T career fields (e.g., computers, math, science, economics, accounting). Psychologically, this can be understood as F types pursuing or crutching their inferior T function.

The same "opposites attract" phenomenon occurs in our relationships. Pairing with our opposite type is really an outer manifestation of our inner desire to permanently secure or integrate our inferior function.

Unfortunately, many people ultimately come to regret decisions that were brokered by their inferior function. They may wish they could have first properly integrated the inferior so as to avoid the need to crutch it externally through a career or relationship.

Phase II also entails significant development and refinement of the auxiliary function. As the second most conscious function, the auxiliary is easier to develop and integrate than the tertiary or inferior. The dominant-auxiliary pairing is generally experienced as more compatible and less polarized than the dominant-inferior duo. The auxiliary function therefore serves as an important bridge between the dominant and inferior function. In many respects, developing and integrating the auxiliary represents an important first step toward the full integration that occurs in Phase III.

Phase III: Integration

Because integration of the functional stack doesn't happen overnight, transitioning to Phase III is often a "two steps forward, one step back" sort of affair. Individuals who enter Phase III have often had their fair share of personal failures, including many associated with the inferior function.

In Phase III, the functions work together in a more supportive and complementary fashion. Rather than leapfrogging between the dominant and inferior functions (e.g., the bipolar behavior seen in Phase II), those in Phase III learn to stay grounded in their dominant function as they explore, develop, and integrate their less conscious functions.

Grounding ourselves in the dominant function means always staying connected to our typological strengths. For instance, it is perfectly healthy for ISTPs to employ their inferior function (Fe) in their interactions with others. But in order to stay grounded, they cannot check their dominant Ti at the door. If ISTPs become engrossed in self-pity, sentimentalism, romantic idealism, or other inferior Fe states, they have typically lost touch with their Ti.

Those in Phase III also become skilled in achieving what psychologist Mihalyi Csikszentmihalyi calls a "flow state." Flow states are characterized by deep absorption in an activity, the optimal amount of challenge and stimulation, and a sense of progress toward a meaningful goal. In a state of flow, we forget about ourselves and our concerns, and "become one with" the activity. The sense of "being in the zone" or "losing track of time" are also characteristic of the flow experience. According to Csikszentmihalyi, most people enjoy the flow state so much that they want to experience it as often as possible.

I think it is entirely reasonable to equate the flow state with the integrated state. Typologically speaking, flow is most likely to occur when we are using our type's strengths and can move fluidly among our functions. In my experience, this tends to occur when performing activities that heavily engage our dominant and auxiliary (and to some extent, tertiary) functions. While the inferior function often supplies some of the interest in, or motivation for, the activity, sustainable flow experiences typically do not entail direct or intensive use of the inferior function. In other words, the inferior function is involved, but in a less overt manner. This allows it to be included and integrated, but in more of a "behind the scenes" sort of way.

Unfortunately, it can at times be easy to confuse a Phase II instance of indulging the inferior function with a Phase III flow state. After all, both can be quite pleasurable and engaging. While the difference between the two is real, it can at times be rather subtle. One difference is Phase II is more apt to involve anxiety, obsessiveness, and/or a spike in adrenaline, whereas Phase III is characterized by a sense of calm and relaxation. Moreover, in Phase II, there is a sense of being gripped by the activity and therefore of not being fully in control of oneself. Those in Phase III, by contrast, feel more in control and are thus less apt to fall into destructive attitudes or behaviors.

Although the nature of an activity plays a role in whether we achieve a state of flow or whether we fall "into the grip" of the inferior function, the state of mind we bring to an activity is equally important. Ideally, the right activity would combine with the proper state of mind to make way for easy and routine obtainment of the integrated flow state.

TYPE PROFILES

INFJ

INFJs are the rarest of the 16 types, constituting only 1-3% of the general population. Unlike INTJs, in which males predominate, there is greater gender parity among INFJs, with near equal numbers of males and females.

INFJs are "old souls." Many grow up feeling wiser than would be predicted by their chronological age. Having discovered the benefits of their Introverted Intuition (Ni) quite early in life, INFJs grow to trust its judgments and insights. Even as children and adolescents, they may find themselves advising and counseling their friends and siblings, or even adult family members. They tend to feel happiest and most fulfilled when helping and enlightening others through their insights.

Because of their strength of intuition (and commensurate detachment from the physical realm), many INFJs report feeling like aliens in the world. One INFJ described her experience as a constant feeling of Deja-Vu. Others report feelings of disembodiment. The fact is that many INFJs (and INTJs) seem to experience the world and their bodies differently than other types do. It is therefore not uncommon for INFJs to question their own sanity.

INFJs see two people in everyone. They see the public persona, the outer shell, which everyone else sees. But more important, their Ni provides a deeper sense or impression people, penetrating appearances and revealing hidden motives and intentions. Consequently, INFJs often feel they can see people more clearly than those people can see themselves.

To best understand INFJs, or other IJ types, it is necessary to recognize the full implications of their dominant function, Introverted Intuition (Ni), being a Perceiving function (see my recent book, *My True Type*, for more on this). Namely, INFJs are far less serious inwardly than they typically appear outwardly. Their inner world is well described as playful, imaginative, colorful, mischievous, and daring. They love playing with ideas, perspectives, theories, images, symbols, and metaphors.

INFJs also enjoy listening to music, watching movies and television, and engaging with people. Perhaps more than anything, they love spending time engrossed in meaningful conversation, which allows them to engage both their Ni and auxiliary Fe functions. One reason INFJs love talking is it affords them the opportunity to help others through their insights. Because of their loquaciousness, INFJs may at times be mistaken for Extraverts.

A signature feature of INFJs (and INTJs) is a deep concern for *quality*. They long to see their Ni ideals materialized in physical reality (Se). Consider the following excerpt from *My True Type*:

> *"While Se attends the appearance of things, Ni is concerned with their deeper qualities and substantiveness . . . While INJs are to some extent concerned with appearances, they are more attuned to the underlying quality and craftsmanship of things . . . ensuring that things are substantive, thoughtfully-crafted, and otherwise amenable to their Ni tastes. NFJs, in particular, often exhibit the most refined (or what other types may deem expensive or pretentious) tastes of all types. The popular television comedy, Frasier, is a great example. Much of the show's humor revolves around the sophisticated snobbiness of Frasier (ENFJ) and his brother Niles (INFJ). This includes*

> *flaunting linguistic formalisms and a high-brow vocabulary, as well as frequent allusions to fine dining, classical music, designer clothing, and the like."*

Like INFPs, INFJs can struggle with depression. This may stem from feeling chronically unheard, useless, or misunderstood. Because Ni perceives the world so differently and profoundly, INFJs often experience a sense of loneliness and isolation, even when they are with other people. Depression may also relate to feeling that their ideals and insights are not being recognized or actualized in the world. They may see the world as deaf to, or unconcerned with, the truths that they have to proclaim. They may therefore question their value in a world that seems indifferent to their insights.

INFJs' Functional Stack & Personality Type Development

INFJs' functional stack is composed of the following functions:

Dominant: Introverted Intuition (Ni)

Auxiliary: Extraverted Feeling (Fe)

Tertiary: Introverted Thinking (Ti)

Inferior: Extraverted Sensing (Se)

Like the other types, INFJs' personality type development can be broadly conceived according to three phases:

Phase I (Childhood)

Phase I of INFJs' type development is characterized by the emergence and differentiation of their dominant function, Introverted Intuition (Ni). As Introverts, they may also show significant development of their auxiliary function, Extraverted Feeling (Fe), which can serve as a helpful extraverted tool for navigating the world of people. The Ni-Fe function pair makes INFJs particularly well-equipped to read and evaluate people, including their underlying motives.

Since Ni is a Perceiving function, it would be wrong to consider INFJs closed-minded at any point in their development. Nonetheless, during Phase I, INFJs can appear more opinionated, closed-minded, or melodramatic. Even if their judgments are precociously accurate, Phase I INFJs may lack some discernment regarding the appropriate time and way to express those judgments. Moreover, their Ni-Fe conclusions have yet to be honed and tempered by their tertiary Ti, making them more reluctant to carefully review or revise them.

Phase II (Adolescence-30s)

Once Ni reaches a certain level of consciousness and differentiation, INFJs' inferior function, Extraverted Sensing (Se), enters the picture and begins to play a more influential and often mischievous role. INFJs are not immune from the dominant-inferior wrestlings described in our Introduction, making this phase as challenging for them as it is for other types. Phase II INFJs may also begin to open up and further refine their judgments by way of their tertiary function, Introverted Thinking (Ti).

Phase III (30s, 40s, & Beyond)

If all goes well and they are fortunate enough to enter Phase III, INFJs become increasingly aware of the insidious ways of their inferior Se. As they become more aware of their inferior and learn to function more authentically as INFJs, they experience greater balance between their Ni and Se. They learn that integrating their Se happens naturally and indirectly as they go about authentically using their Ni and Fe. As they cultivate conditions that support their natural strengths, Phase

III INFJs come to experience a heightened sense of peace, wholeness, and satisfaction.

INFJs' Dominant Function: Introverted Intuition (Ni)

Intuition is generally considered a subconscious process. It is often contrasted with more conscious types of rational thought. Because Intuition is commonly associated with the unconscious, it is often thought to have a certain magical quality, capable of delivering comprehensive answers or solutions suddenly—"out of the blue."

One of the central features of Intuition is its capacity to synthesize information. It is sensitive to patterns and similarities, quickly seeing connections among disparate pieces of data. By seeing how everything is connected and interrelated, it is capable of discerning universal laws and structures.

What is interesting about types with dominant Intuition, including INFJs, is that this Intuitive process, which for non-Intuitives is largely unconscious, is more accessible and observable in consciousness. This seems particularly true for INTJs and INFJs, whose Intuition is directly inwardly rather than being fused with the outside world. INJs have the good fortune of witnessing and consciously participating in a mysterious process which for other types is entirely unconscious.

Because Ni affords INFJs a more intimate relationship with the workings of what most people call the subconscious mind, INFJs' routine existence often assumes a sort of dreamlike quality. For INFJs, there is less of a distinction between their ordinary waking state and the experience of sleep. At times, this can make it difficult to separate dream from reality, making nightmares all the more disturbing for this type. It is little wonder that many INJs, including Jung himself, find dream analysis so intriguing and important.

Because of their ready access to subconscious or subliminal information, INFJs are commonly viewed as profound, insightful, and sometimes even psychic or prophetic. While not diminishing the unique capacities of INFJs, Ni can be rational, non-magical terms.

In order to understand Ni, it is first necessary to understand INFJ's inferior function, Extraverted Sensing (Se). For INFJs, Se functions subconsciously and is constantly gathering copious amounts of sensory information from the environment. Meanwhile, their Ni is constantly working to process and synthesize this incoming data, like assembling pieces of a puzzle. Eventually, it manages to construct an impression or vision of what is happening. Because other types are not privy to the workings of this Ni-Se processing loop, it can seem as though INFJs' insights are magical or divinely inspired. In reality, INFJs cannot see the future, but are simply more skilled than most at accurately discerning what is happening in a given situation. This allows them to better envision how things might unfold should they continue along their current course. This ability to accurately "see" is why INFJs are sometimes described as prophets or seers.

It is often said that human beings rely more heavily on vision than we do our other senses. This seems especially true of INFJs, who often ascribe a strong visual element to their Ni. INFJs often "think" by way of images rather than words. Their intuitions often manifest in the form of symbols, images, dreams, or patterns. This is consistent with Jung's characterization of the Ni type as a dreamer or seer. There is a distinct visual character to these notions, which is why vision-related terms—*foresight, insight, seer, visionary*, etc.—are invariably used in describing INFJs. The visual nature of Ni might also tie into INFJs' inferior Se, which is also a highly visual function. The difference is that Se is attuned to the specifics and details of the environment, whereas Ni is more concerned with forming an impression or theory of what is happening based on the totality of incoming sensory information.

INFJs' propensity for processing information visually may contribute to one of their signature strengths: reconciling opposites. One advantage of visual processing is it doesn't have the same rules or impediments of verbal processing. In some cases, problems may be better solved by employing images or symbols rather than by other means. It should not surprise us that Jung himself hailed the value of imagery and symbols. For Jung, symbols were critical for dealing with paradoxes, including the challenge of reconciling opposing psychological functions, which he dubbed "the type problem."

INFJs' Auxiliary Function: Extraverted Feeling (Fe)

INFJs use Extraverted Feeling (Fe) as their auxiliary function. As the most interpersonal of all the functions, Fe is attuned to surveying and improving interpersonal feelings and morale. Like other FJ types, INFJs work to cultivate "good feelings" in the interpersonal environment. In order to survey others' feelings, Fe contributes to INFJs' ability to read emotional expressions and body language. This, in combination with their Se and Ni, allow them to effectively read, understand, and relate to others.

Interestingly, INFJs can have a more difficult time with perceiving and understanding their own emotions. This is due to the fact that their Feeling function is directed outwardly (i.e., extraverted) rather than inwardly. Unlike INFPs, whose Feeling function is introverted (Fi), INFJs are less equipped to manage their emotions independently. Inwardly, they deal in the currency of Intuition (Ni) and Thinking (Ti). Hence, when INFJs find themselves in emotionally taxing circumstances, they often turn to others for aid and support.

Fe also entails an extraversion of judgment. INFJs utilize their Fe to express their thoughts, feelings, opinions, and grievances. Fe gives voice and shape to INFJs' feelings and intuitions. In many cases, INFJs do not fully understand the nature of an Ni insight until given the opportunity to verbalize it. They may have a hunch or a gut feeling, but the content of the intuition can remain somewhat nebulous until it is expressed via their Fe. Assuming they have not been severely censored in their upbringing, INFJs are generally happy to share their feelings and perspectives. In fact, given the right opportunity, INFJs will often talk at length about their feelings and intuitions. Unlike FP types, who generally prefer a more dialogical format, INFJs are inclined toward monologues, which allow them to fully flesh out their ideas on a certain topic.

INFJs' Fe can present differently among strangers than it does with their intimates. In larger groups, INFJs may seem consistently cheery as part of their attempt to cultivate good feelings. Many INFJs have a good sense of humor and can be funny and engaging. Enlisting their vivid imaginations and knack for metaphor, they can also make good storytellers. In the company of close confidants, however, INFJs use their Fe to be more open and direct with their grievances. Since some INFJs feel like tortured souls, their commentary may take on a characteristically negative tone. They may seem moody, pessimistic, discontented, or restless. They can also seem fairly intense in their communication when infused with the emotion of Fe. Consequently, their expressions can seem exaggerated, dramatic, or irrational, especially to Thinking types. They differ in this respect from INFPs, who are less disposed to melodrama in their verbiage. INFJs can also be susceptible to self-pity and self-loathing, seeing themselves as victims. They may curse the fact that life isn't fair, feeling that they always end up with the short end of the stick.

For INFJs, expressing themselves through their Fe is critical to their psychological and physical health and well-being. Even if doing so does not provide them with immediate solutions to the problem at hand, they tend to feel better once they have expressed their feelings, whether through words or tears. This is especially important for the mates or friends of INFJs to recognize. While not necessarily looking for others to solve their problems, INFJs value emotional support, empathy, and reassurance. Without such an outlet, INFJs can begin to feel isolated and depressed, turning to their inner fantasy world as a means of escape. And while fantasizing may seem helpful in the short-term, it can make the real world seem even less tolerable and exacerbate existing frustrations toward life.

Even if not to the same extent as EFJs, INFJs can be warm, welcoming, loyal, giving, and self-sacrificing. At the same time, as Introverts, they need time to themselves to recharge their proverbial batteries. This creates an ongoing, even lifelong, struggle for INFJs, trying to balance their own needs and desires with those of others.

INFJs may also experience value conflicts between their Ni and Fe. For example, they may be asked by a friend or relative to donate to a cause they don't believe in. This puts them in the difficult position of deciding between honoring their own perspectives (Ni) and maintaining the harmony of the relationship (Fe). Since INFJs can have difficulty saying no, they will often opt to oblige others, even while inwardly regretting doing so. INFJs may experience similar issues in school. On the one hand, they are disposed to questioning the veracity of what the teacher or other students are saying, not to mention issues of character. On the other hand, they want to please the teacher and maintain external harmony. This can leave them feeling torn between their allegiance to truth (Ni) and to people (Fe).

Because of the strength of their Fe, INFJs need to be careful not to abandon their Ni in the face of outward pressures. Since Ni is their best and most reliable compass for navigating life, when they lose track of it, INFJs can easily feel lost, restless, and frustrated. Hence, when it comes to decision-making, INFJs are wise to listen primarily to their own inner voice.

INFJs' Tertiary Function: Introverted Thinking (Ti)

The role of Introverted Thinking (Ti) in INFJs is to open and further refine their Fe judgments. Ti can help INFJs think more critically and analytically. It can serve as an aid and check to their Ni-Fe, helping them discern where their ideas might fit into existing categories and frameworks of knowledge. It adds an element of logic that is less apparent in the earlier phases of their type development. For instance, INFJs who grew up in a religious home may be disposed to interpreting their insights through the lens of their childhood faith tradition. As they develop their Ti, however, they might come to question whether that wisdom might be better understood in psychological terms.

What INFJs may perceive as a negative or difficult feature of their Ti is its tendency to generate self-doubt. As Ti butts up against the insights offered by their Ni, INFJs may temporarily distrust their most cherished and utilized mode of knowing—their Intuition. But personal growth is never easy, not for any type. With time, INFJs settle into a healthy balance between their Ni and Ti, intuitively knowing how to apply their Ti without spoiling the insights proffered by their Intuition.

Less developed INFJs may see little need to use or develop their Ti. Since their Ni-Fe pairing provides them with strong convictions about truth, taking an additional step to Ti may seem unnecessary. With time and maturity, however, INFJs can grow increasingly comfortable with their Ti and recognize its inherent value.

INFJs' Inferior Function: Extraverted Sensing (Se)

As is true for other types, INFJs are prone to experience a protracted power struggle between their dominant and inferior function (i.e., Phase II of type development), one which often entails significant pain and hardship. Fortunately, this hardship can be minimized by gaining a better understanding of their inferior function, Extraverted Sensing (Se), as well as potential ways of integrating it.

Generally speaking, the inferior nature of Se makes INFJs less naturally attuned to the concrete details or physical elements of life. While their Se takes in plenty of sensory data about the physical world, this information is synthesized and experienced through the lens of intuition (Ni). So instead of noticing specifics about people or the environment, INFJs are more apt to experience what we might call an *impression.* They get a general sense (i.e., intuition) of people or things, such as whether an individual seems psychospiritually healthy or unhealthy. While INFJs are experts when it comes to these sorts of general impressions, they can be rather oblivious to external specifics and details (Se).

In experiencing the world through the filter of Ni, INFJs often report a perpetual sense of déjà vu or strange alienation with respect to their physical surroundings. One of our INFJ readers described it this way:

> *"I will literally just be sitting at dinner and suddenly realize that I am a physical being in a room surrounded by so many things I didn't realize for the past hour. This can be a confusing and frightening experience."*

This is not to say that INFJs are unaffected by their environs. As "highly sensitive persons (HSPs)," their nervous system is highly permeable and sensitive to all sorts of stimuli. This can make them more susceptible to being overwhelmed or overstimulated than other types. In some cases, because of their N-S disconnect, they may not realize that they are overstimulated until it's too late.

I observed one INFJ, for instance, who seemed to be enjoying herself at a rather loud, strobe light laden concert. But not long after it was over, she experienced a debilitating headache and what seemed to be a "crash" of her nervous system. Somehow, she had managed to remain unaware of the sensory overload until she was effectively incapacitated by it.

INFJs report similar experiences with extended shopping excursions. While they may enjoy themselves for a while, sustained use of Se (i.e., browsing), combined with the noise and commotion of crowds, can result in a subconscious sensory overload or exhaustion that eventually catches up with them.

In short, INFJs have a tenuous relationship with the physical environment. Not only can the S world seem quite strange and foreign to them, but if they are not careful, it can overwhelm them. This is why INFJs, especially as children, can be leery of new S experiences, such as trying new foods or physical actions. Intuitively realizing their tenuous grasp on the S world, they tend to "error on the safe side."

As adults, however, INFJs may gradually open themselves to new S experiences. I have known a number of INFJs, for instance, who are bona fide "foodies," seeing every meal as an opportunity to experience new sensual delights. This points to the love-hate relationship that all types have with the inferior function. Depending on the circumstances, inferior function experiences may be perceived as scary, stressful, blissful, or intriguing.

Impracticality

The inferior nature of their Se also makes INFJs the most impractical of all types, especially with respect to ST matters. This is partly due to their ST obliviousness and partly to their desire to remain in their inner N world and to ignore certain S duties.

Because of their ST shortcomings, INFJs are prone to struggle with subsistence-related fears. Feeling that ST matters are in many respects beyond their sphere of control, they may fret about things like losing their job or not having enough money. INFJ parents may fear that their obliviousness to physical reality might somehow compromise the safety or well-being of their children.

To compensate, INFJs may turn to other types to help them handle life's S details. This can allay their S fears and help them feel okay about remaining in their N playground. Unfortunately, society is not always sympathetic to this sort of arrangement, perhaps seeing the INFJ as lazy, incompetent, or too weak to handle the pressures of life.

On a lighter note, INFJs may also showcase their impractical nature in their wardrobe choices. They may, for instance, own 20 pairs of high heels but not a single pair of comfortable walking shoes, perhaps ascribing it to their concern for "style over comfort." Or, they may live in a rather sparsely furnished living space due to difficulties either finding the "right" furnishings or having inadequate funds to purchase them. Unlike NFPs, they are typically unwilling to settle for hodgepodge or makeshift options. For INFJs, something either fits with their overall Ni vision or it doesn't. Settling for something less than ideal is not an option.

Mind-Body Disconnect

Another way in which Sensing is "missing" from INFJs' typical experience is their disconnectedness with their own body. One of our INFJ readers described his experience this way:

> *"I regularly forget to eat, or put it off because of the effort it takes to prepare sustenance or because it may detract from the pleasure of being in my mind . . . I don't like to physically "do" much of anything. It is also very startling for me to be touched without invitation, which seems to jerk me out of my mind and forces me to pay attention to sensation. There are also times I try to grasp my present reality and suddenly feel afraid. I look around and think, "I am in this body . . . in this house . . . with these walls . . . around these people . . . and they are my family . . . who are these people?" Thinking about these things can upset my stomach or may even cause me to hyperventilate. It's not that I don't love my family. It's just when I try to focus on the here and now, it can be pretty terrifying, as if I'm an ancient being suddenly waking up in someone else's body."*

Elaine Schallock, in her article, "How INJs Approach their Body and Physical Needs," put it this way:

> *"For INJs there is an extreme level of distrust, even demonization, of the body and its processes because S remains so alien and out of the INJ's control. Physiological responses are not well understood and often not accurately perceived; even supposedly "pleasurable" physiological feelings are regularly repressed and/or dismissed as unwanted. So-called "thrill seeking" which brings up butterflies of excitement for other types can be a source of anguish for Ni types who may experience that bodily response as pain, nausea, or dizziness . . ."*

Schallock continues:

> *"Long-term physical suffering is seen as the epitome of the worst kind of evil and the deepest of their fears. If this occurs, INJs are likely to go into an extreme state of grip behavior as they are poorly equipped to deal with acute physical pain. They may become angry and incredulous, convinced that the body is lashing out against them somehow. Some INJs react by becoming positively punitive, putting themselves with even more physical stress by doing things like slamming back a potentially unsafe dose of NSAIDS or exercising to the point of injury. They tend not to react gently or respectfully toward the body, blaming and disciplining when things go awry."*

Clearly, S difficulties can transport INFJs into a dark place, one that may involve turning against themselves (i.e., against their own bodies) in extreme or unhealthy ways.[1] In trying to compensate for this mind-body disconnect, INFJs may subject themselves to regimens (sometimes severe or harsh) of diet, exercise, and medical check-ups. Without these sorts of structures and checkpoints in place, they may worry that their mind-body disconnect might precipitate, or render them oblivious to, a potentially serious health crisis.

S, N, and Work

One of the most difficult realities for INFJs is that, in order for their Ni to work optimally, their Se needs must first be adequately satisfied. In other words, the potency of their Ni to some extent rests on their S livelihood.

This is typically not a problem for INFJs as children, since their S subsistence is supplied by their parents. But once INFJs hit adulthood and are expected to "fend for themselves," they are suddenly faced with a more difficulty reality. Namely, while INFJs would love to get paid for their Ni talents, they feel they must first have a stable S platform to stand on. Ideally, such a platform would not only meet their basic subsistence needs, but would also satisfy their aesthetic preferences and their need for a safe and quiet setting. Now if INFJs happen to choose rewarding Ni-Fe work from the get-go (e.g., counseling), work that also happens to be financially generous, then they may be lucky enough to circumvent this problem. But those who choose either the wrong career or one with lower pay may loathe the fact that some sort of serious sacrifice must be made. In this situation, they may feel forced to either take a higher-paying, but ultimately less satisfying job, or to suffer ongoing S deficits that may hamstring their N productivity.

Aesthetics and Perfectionism

INFJs are aesthetes. They love beautiful things and are sensitive to the aesthetics of their surroundings. As dominant Ns, this is often experienced as sensitivity to ambience, that is, to the general mood or impression of a given setting.

Unlike NFPs, who typically display more Bohemian or eclectic tastes, INFJs gravitate toward more formal, structured, and "themed" spaces. When vacationing, for instance, NFPs are typically satisfied with inexpensive or makeshift options, such as camping, hostels, or affordable hotels. INFJs (or ENFJs), by contrast, will gravitate toward more posh or formal accommodations, such as four or five-star hotels. While NFPs like the quirky and casual, NFJs prefer the fine and formal. Again, the television show Frasier is a good, even if somewhat hyperbolic, example of INFJs' lifestyle preferences.

Although INFJs are most concerned with the overall feel of a space, they also recognize that the whole is made up of parts. So what typically happens is INFJs discern a general vision or theme for their living environment, and then gradually work to populate that vision with individual pieces. While the vision (Ni) part typically comes rather easily to INFJs, materializing it and filling in its details (Se) almost always proves more difficult and stressful. Indeed, this is where INFJs' notorious perfectionism is apt to rear its head. This is also why making art can be a stressful affair for INFJs, as they struggle to perfectly materialize (Se) their Ni vision. Some INFJs may sacrifice everything, even their own health, to ensure their vision finds a perfect incarnation. In such a state of mind, even the smallest deviation from their ideal may feel like the end of the world.

In her article, "The "Other Side" of the INFJ," Elaine Schallock suggests that INFJs are particularly apt to fall prey to their perfectionistic dark side when their work is on public display. She gives the following example:

> *"An INFJ responsible for planning a large wedding anniversary party for her parents does everything in her power in the planning mode to make sure the soiree is beautifully prepared and others are comfortable and happy. The INFJ's power of visualization is incredible thanks to Ni; in the INFJ's mind's eye she can see how the tables are laid out, the music, the mood, the invitations, etc. But when the big day comes and the food arrives late, the weather is unbearably hot, and the people are cranky, the INFJ (who of course didn't consider a "back-up" plan – this would*

> *have been far too practical) becomes frustrated, emotional, and stressed out. There is a tendency to take personal responsibility for such Se failures. The INFJ figures if she had only planned it better somehow this might have been avoided. The entire "disaster" is perceived as a personal attack on the INFJ's inferior function, her ST "blindspots," and ultimately her ego. For those unfortunate souls attempting to console the INFJ dealing with such a letdown, there can be an equal sense of frustration. Once the INFJ's vision fails to come to fruition and she falls into the grip of her inferior function, acting logically goes out the window. Instead of being open to a modification of the plan, the INFJ holds on ever more tightly to the original vision, feeling as though this is the only way to correct the problem. The INFJ is then caught in a paradox. To sacrifice the Ni vision would mean giving up the dominant function, the very center of her "sense of self." She is, understandably, loathe to do so. But ultimately what the INFJ must realize is that this is an illusion. What is touted as a commitment to the Ni vision is really a veiled commitment to the Se outcome. Of course, the line between Se and Ni is incredibly thin (where does an object end and the concept behind it begin?), which accounts for the ease by which they accidentally fall prey to such illusions."*

According to Schallock, INFJs' obsession with Se outcomes, that is, with the perfect materialization of what they see as good, true, and/or beautiful, as well as their tendency to impugn themselves for any shortcoming in this respect, can be their downfall. In her view, this perfectionistic mindset stems from INFJs trying to shortcut their way to wholeness by jumping from Ni to Se ("jumping the stack") rather than moving from Ni to Fe. In other words, INFJs effectively bypass their judging functions (Fe and Ti) in favor of remaining in what amounts to a perpetual state of perception (i.e., Ni and Se). Schallock suggests this state of perfectionistic perceiving is particularly common among INFJ artists, especially visual artists, as they strive to perfectly replicate (Se) mental images (Ni).

Integration

Instead of jumping the stack, Schallock suggests that INFJs are wise to take up work that encourages them to move from Ni to Fe. This leads INFJs to function more like analysts or interpreters, proffering (Fe) their impressions (Ni) of things (either verbally or in writing), as well as what might unfold if things continue on their current trajectory.

In so doing, INFJs can relinquish some measure of responsibility for seeing that actual change occurs (Se). They can do their part as "readers of the situation," and then trust other types (e.g., S types) to heed and act on their analysis. By releasing themselves from Se responsibility and trusting that others will do their part, INFJs can free themselves from the debilitating stress and pressure of trying to perfect or beautify the world.

The Star Wars character Yoda is a good, even if idealized, example of a healthy INFJ. Yoda's main task is to function as an intuitive observer, to keep tabs, by way of the force (i.e., intuition), on the moral landscape of the galaxy. But he does not restrict himself to only perceiving. When others seek him out for advice, or when he senses that a situation is dire, he issues the appropriate insights or directives. After saying his piece, he then returns to a state of perceiving until his insights are once again required. While he occasionally acts (Se), such as engaging in an occasional (and admittedly gripping) light-saber duel, this is never his first preference; physical action is always a last resort.

In sum, INFJs must learn that, despite the allure of doing so, engaging their inferior function directly, such as through S action, is not the path to their salvation. While directly engaging their Se may appear to be the quickest and easiest way of integrating it, this is really more of a trap or illusion. The longer, but ultimately more sustainable and reliable path to integration, is moving from Ni to Fe. As is true for other types, it is the oft-overlooked auxiliary function that represents their first big step toward wholeness.

Notes

1. It would be fairly unusual for INFPs to respond to their body in this sort of way since Sensing is not their least conscious function. By way of their tertiary Si, INFPs tend to feel more attuned to their bodies, which they often augment through mind-body practices such as yoga.

INTJ

INTJs' signature strength is deep perception. They are naturally attuned to "the big picture" and cannot help but see how everything is interconnected. Their ability to perceive deep patterns and causal relationships has helped many INTJs achieve eminence in science, mathematics, and other theory-centered occupations.

Although INTJs are classified as Thinking types, their dominant function is Intuition, or more specifically, Introverted Intuition (Ni). In seeing the world through Ni lenses, their typical mode of operation is well described as impressionistic. Rather than noticing or concerning themselves with the details of the world around them, their existence is more cerebral or dreamlike. This can lead them to feel estranged from their physical environs, not to mention their own bodies.

While INTJs may be relatively unaware of how others perceive them, their "other-worldliness" often earns them labels such as quirky, awkward, nerdy, or oblivious. Onlookers sense that INTJs seem to "live in their own world." Immersed in their own minds and interests, INTJs can be oblivious to social norms or other practical aspects of life. While incredibly "book smart," they may fall short when it comes to social or "street smarts."

At some point in their lives, INTJs start to take notice of how characteristically different they are from their peers. They may even joke about their own nerdy or esoteric interests. Fortunately, they can usually find a few friends with overlapping interests, even if those friendships are maintained through what others might consider non-social activities, such as playing video games over the internet.

Further complicating INTJs' social life is their use of Extraverted Thinking (Te). The majority of males, at least in the United States, are TP types, all of who use Extraverted Feeling (Fe) rather than Te. This gives TPs (including INTPs) a leg up when it comes to casually connecting with others in social situations. TPs often enjoy social situations (at least for a stint), which grant them opportunities to showcase or sharpen their social chops. By contrast, INTJs, along with other Te types, often loathe unfamiliar social situations. They find it painfully difficult to "rub elbows" or engage in any measure of "small talk" with strangers. This further intensifies their sense of being "different" from their peers.

INTJs also have a reputation for being "walking encyclopedias." They are sponges for all sorts of information, be it historical, scientific, technical, or otherwise. I've met many INTJs who seem to have "photographic memories," able to recall nearly anything they've been exposed to. One of my INTJ friends, for instance, readily recites lines from movies he's only seen once.

In recognizing their powers of insight (Ni), not to mention their vast stores of factual knowledge (Te), INTJs are naturally inclined to share what they know with others. In addition to activities such as gaming, dispensing ideas or information is one of the easiest ways for INTJs to engage with others. They enjoy opportunities to utilize their typological strengths and enlighten others. Unfortunately, this can sometimes result in INTJs being misconstrued as arrogant "know-it-alls."

Despite their introverted status, INTJs can be surprisingly talkative. Like INFJs, they can talk at great length (and depth) on topics that interest them. This is one reason INTJs often enjoy the role of lecturer or professor. And while they are rarely the most dynamic or energetic of orators, INTJs are typically decent story-tellers and good for occasional injections of droll humor or cultural references. This can help humanize them in the eyes of their audience, even if their overall delivery remains a bit dry or mechanical.

Because INTJs extravert their Thinking judgments (i.e., Te), others commonly (and often wrongly) assume them to be characteristically serious individuals. This misses the fact that they are dominant Perceivers (i.e., their dominant Ni function is a Perceiving function), which makes them far more inwardly easygoing, even playful, than most people realize. I've known some INTJs who begin every day with comedy, such as catching up on the latest "9gag" website postings. This is one reason type theory is so important: it keys us into inner (I) – outer (E) type differences that might otherwise be overlooked.

Another consequence of INTJs' Perceiving dominance is their tendency to be passive or phlegmatic. More proactive types, such as ENTJs, might even consider them a bit lazy or apathetic. But calling INTJs lazy is to miss the point of what it means to be a Perceiver. Namely, since INTJs' first and foremost job is to Perceive rather than Judge or act, functioning in a passive mode of perception is actually their most authentic mode of operating. Indeed, the reason that INTJs' theories and insights are often superior is because they do not force things. They patiently allow their Ni intuition to collect and synthesize all the pertinent information before they draw conclusions. Again, others may be blinded to this reality if they focus exclusively on INTJs' external presentation.

INTJs' Functional Stack & Type Development

Each personality type prefers to use four of the eight functions first described by Jung. These four functions comprise a type's "functional stack." The relative strength of preference for these four functions is expressed in the following manner: dominant, auxiliary, tertiary, and inferior. INTJs' first preference is Ni, followed by Te, Fi and Se respectively. This is depicted in the arrangement of their functional stack:

Dominant: Introverted Intuition (Ni)

Auxiliary: Extraverted Thinking (Te)

Tertiary: Introverted Feeling (Fi)

Inferior: Extraverted Sensing (Se)

While we will soon discuss each of these functions in greater depth, for now, we will turn our attention to another feature of INTJs' personality— their type development. As is true for all the personality types, INTJs' type development consists of three general phases. These phases roughly correspond to the ordering of the functional stack, with Ni being the first function to blossom, Te the second, on so on. But as we will see, the inferior function is sort of a special case, summoning INTJs' attention at an earlier phase than might otherwise be expected.

Phase I (Childhood)

Early in life, Introverted Intuition (Ni) emerges as INTJs' dominant function. The degree to which the dominant function needs to be worked on or developed is not entirely clear. If one can argue, for instance, that great athletes are born not made, might the same not be true for a type's dominant function?

Regardless, INTJs' amass a great deal of information for their Ni to chew on throughout their childhood. The longer they live and the more they see, the more their worldview crystallizes and the more confident they feel in their understanding of things. Even young INTJs are keen to understand what is happening around them. This is what Ni does. It looks beyond appearances to discern the root causes and structures of things.

But as we've seen, INTJs aren't always all that serious-minded. Many spend their childhood playing video games, watching movies, learning an instrument, or surfing the web. They acquire much of their knowledge through happenstance, without much in the way of conscious effort.

Phase II (Adolescence-30s)

In Phase II, their inferior function, Extraverted Sensing (Se), begins to assert itself and to play a more prominent role in INTJs' psychic drama. The inferior's undue influence can be seen as stemming from its bipolar relationship with the dominant function. Namely, in order to ensure psychological diversity or balance, INTJs feel compelled to experience something characteristically distinct from the dominant function. The inferior function is often experienced as magical, mysterious, and exciting, even blissful. Some have described it as "a whole new world." It can thereby serve as a powerful source of energy and motivation. This is why all types, especially those in Phase II, display a strong appetite for, and curiosity toward, their inferior function.

As will be enumerated in our forthcoming section on Se, the emergence of Se may take the form of INTJs' showing greater interest in novel aesthetic or sensory (S) experiences. While INTJ children are often leery of new experiences, as time goes on, they may gradually open themselves to S novelties. Although INTJs tend not to be as "experimental" in their approach to life as NPs, many come to welcome new S experiences as an invigorating alternative to their typical state of NT cerebralism.

Because of its deep allure and sense of novelty, the inferior can lead INTJs, to make questionable career or relationship decisions in

Phase II. It may, for instance, cause them to pair with incompatible types under the spell of the "opposites attract" (i.e., inferior function attraction) phenomenon. Therefore, Phase II INTJs can typically benefit from a reality check, remembering that their "core self" is ultimately founded on their Ni, not Se.

The siren call of the inferior function can be effectively counterbalanced by regular use and development of the auxiliary function. For INTJs, this means bringing a greater measure of Te to the proverbial table. Te helps INTJs rationally explicate their intuitions, whether in math, science, consulting, or related fields. Regular employment of Te also encourages INTJs to move out of Perceiving mode and into Judging, promoting a more diverse and balanced personality.

Phase III (30s, 40s, & Beyond)

Phase III INTJs wise up to the tricks and temptations of the inferior function, discovering more sustainable ways of integrating their functions. Rather than leapfrogging between the dominant and inferior functions (e.g., the bipolar behavior characteristic of Phase II), they learn to stay grounded in their Ni as they explore, develop, and integrate their less conscious functions.

INTJs in Phase III also become skilled in achieving what psychologist Mihalyi Csikszentmihalyi has dubbed the "flow state." Flow states are characterized by deep absorption in an activity, an optimal balance of challenge and stimulation, and a sense of progress toward a meaningful goal. In a state of flow, INTJs forget about themselves and their concerns, "becoming one with" the activity. Flow states are most likely to emerge when INTJs perform activities that engage their dominant and auxiliary functions.

INTJs' Dominant Function: Introverted Intuition (Ni)

As we saw earlier, in order to best understand INTJs, we must recognize the full implications of their dominant function, Ni, being a Perceiving function. While INTJs can certainly function as rational thinkers via their auxiliary Te, their first preference is to process matters in less rational ways a la Ni.

In its popular connotation, intuition is understood as an unconscious way of knowing, or what writer Malcolm Gladwell has cleverly described as "thinking without thinking." It is therefore interesting to consider that, for dominant Intuitives such as INTJs, intuition is understood to be their most *conscious* function. While it is true that intuition is more conscious for INTJs than it is for other types, we must remember that Ni is a Perceiving function. So although INTJs may have readier access to its workings and products, there is still a sense in which they don't really control it. Intuitive insight often seems to emerge *ex nihilo*, as a welcomed but unexpected gift from the muses.

With that said, INTJs do possess some measure of control over the types of problems they want their Ni to solve, not to mention the raw material they feed into it. The more they immerse themselves in a certain problem or subject matter, the more their insight will deepen. So it's not that INTJs can be totally hands-off and allow Ni to do all the heavy lifting for them. Healthy INTJs find the right balance between allowing their Ni to do its thing and consciously participating with the process.

Because of its prescience and depth of insight, Ni may at times seem to border on magical or supernatural. While not discounting it impressiveness, the Ni process can, at least to some extent, be rationally explicated. Namely, INTJs' inferior function, Extraverted Sensing (Se), unconsciously collects vast quantities of sensory information from the outside world. This data is then kindly forwarded to Ni, which tries to make sense of it, like assembling the pieces of a puzzle.

Eventually, an impression is formed that reveals the deeper reality or N pattern behind the data.

It is often said that human beings rely more heavily on vision than their other senses. This seems particularly true of INJ types, who often associate a strong visual element with their Ni. Many report thinking by way of images more than words. Their intuitions may take the form of symbols, images, dreams, or patterns. This is consistent with Jung's characterization of the Ni type as the dreamer or seer. There is a distinct visual character to these notions, which is why vision-related terms—*foresight, insight, seer, visionary*, etc.—are commonly ascribed to INJs.

Visual processing may prove advantageous for solving problems that seem resistant to rational solutions. This is because visual processing isn't bound by the same rules or limitations as verbal or logical processing. Indeed, Ni's unique approach to problem-solving may explain why INTJs often make such formidable analysts and theorists.

INTJs' Auxiliary Function: Extraverted Thinking (Te)

While Ni is a holistic and synthesizing function, INTJs' auxiliary function, Te, hails squarely from the left side of the brain. The left hemisphere is characteristically logical, abstract, analytical, and systematic. It breaks things down into their constituent parts, names those parts, explicates their functions, and determines their relationships to other parts.

A Te-based approach also emphasizes quantification, as well as the establishment of measurable goals and standards. Never vague or ambiguous, it employs clear definitions, policies, plans, and procedures. It carefully spells out how to get from here to there, using as many maps, directions, and labels as necessary. The ultimate goal of Te is to render things logically intelligible, making them more amenable to human manipulation, prediction, and control.

Ni is neither characteristically rational nor highly systematic. Only the Judging functions, most notably Te, operate in such a fashion. And because Ni comes first in INTJs' functional stack, Te is ultimately more of a servant than a master. It is primarily used to analyze or flesh out Ni's intuitions. Once an intuition has formed, Te takes the reins and works to give it rational form, sort of like decompressing a computer file. Te's ability to translate intuitions into words, diagrams, or formulae is important because it helps others better comprehend INTJs' insights.

In explicating their intuitions, Te is highly systematic and methodical, even perfectionistic. INTJs pay close attention to the way things are ordered, ensuring that their work follows the appropriate linear or logical sequencing. They may also work to incorporate relevant Te facts, data, and other objective considerations.

With that said, INTJs always keep at least one eye on the bigger picture, ensuring that they are staying true to their foundational intuition. This is one way INTJs differ from SJ types, who often miss the bigger picture or end up getting lost in the particulars. Not only are INTJs blessed with the ability to isolate and analyze specifics, but they simultaneously maintain a clear vision of the whole system, including its hierarchical structure and the interrelationships of its component parts.

The fact that INTJs lead with Ni rather than Te also casts doubt on perceptions of INTJs being excessively stubborn or closed-minded. Such perceptions are typically rooted in observations of INTJs' extraversion of Thinking. But because Te closure is not their typical or preferred state of being, we should be careful not to confuse their outer presentation (Te) with their inner reality (Ni). INTJs are far more open inwardly than they may seem outwardly.

Another feature of Te, which we touched on earlier, is its social presentation. Unlike Fe, Te is not concerned with procuring social harmony or group morale. It is characteristically impersonal—focused on facts, objects, and systems rather than feelings. The inability of others to approach things impersonally or objectively is a common point of frustration for INTJs. They may feel incredulous toward others' repeated failure to see, and/or appropriately respond to, objective truth. INTJs often feel that, regardless of how sound their arguments or the amount of evidence they present, some people simply won't budge. Even more frustrating is when they see those same people responding to F influences. When this happens repeatedly, INTJs may become dismayed or nihilistic, concerned that humanity will forever remain blind to the truth.

One can see this playing out in the political careers of INTJs Hillary Clinton and Al Gore. Both are among the most intelligent of politicians, possessing a solid understanding of national and global dynamics. But both are/were plagued by a lack of charisma and likeability (i.e., a lack of Fe), making it difficult for them to inspire or connect with others on an emotional level.

INTJs' Tertiary Function: Introverted Feeling (Fi)

Despite their preference for Te over Fi, it would be a mistake to assume that INTJs are emotionless robots. The real difficulty for INTJs is that, regardless of how strong their emotions or convictions may be, this often gets lost in translation. We know that INTJs' feelings don't readily translate because their preferred Feeling function (Fi) is introverted in its direction. Instead of extraverting Feeling, they extravert Thinking (Te). This precludes others from readily accessing their emotional state. Instead of seeing variations of expression or intonation (Fe), one encounters a relatively flat, monochromatic presentation (Te).

With respect to other people, Fi is associated with intensive emotional investments in a limited number of individuals. Instead of distributing its emotional energies broadly in the way of Fe, Fi is more focused and discriminating. This is why INTJs typically show little interest in social networking. Instead, they typically invest themselves emotionally in their families, along with one or two close friends. They tend to be loyal and committed partners, as well as unswervingly devoted to the well-being of their children. While they may be skeptical toward a great many things, the value of family and friendship is typically not one of them.

Career-wise, Fi may inspire INTJs to work toward social change and reform, be it in business, politics, economics, education, or otherwise. Fi is highly sensitive to injustices, especially those affecting individuals perceived to be incapable of helping or defending themselves (e.g., children, the elderly, the poor, etc.). Hence, INTJs' Fi often teams up with Ni to foresee paths to a more just and equitable world. Te may also play a role in the process, such as developing strategic or logistical plans for reforming broken systems. This combination of Ni, Te, and Fi explains why INTJs often score high on the Enneagram's type One, often called "The Reformer."

With that said, I've observed a fair amount of variability among INTJs with respect to the prominence of Fi in their personality. I know one INTJ, for instance, who had a rather difficult upbringing and has spent most of his adult life trying to understand and remediate his childhood wounds. This led him to develop interests in both normal and abnormal psychology. I've also known INTJs who show little more than a passing interest in psychology. It may be that differences in childhood experiences affect the degree to which INTJs focus on Fi matters, including their own emotional landscape. The interaction of nature and nurture may also affect the degree of INTJs' emotional stability. Some INTJs are emotionally labile and constantly turning to others for support. Other INTJs are characteristically more steady and independent in handling their emotions.

The last thing I'll mention about INTJs' Fi is its contribution to their interest in self-knowledge, including their desire to understand what makes them unique and different. For quite some time, I was perplexed as to why so many INTJs took interest in personality typology. I hypothesized that in most cases it was probably career-related, such as trying to match their personality to a particular career field. I later realized that their reasons often ran deeper than that. Namely, similar to what we see in FP types, INTJs' Fi compels them to understand who they are as unique individuals.

INTJs' Inferior Function: Extraverted Sensing (Se)

The importance of the inferior function has long been grossly underestimated in the type community. Sometimes called the lost, missing, or repressed function, it is the most unconscious of the four functions. It is also the most difficult to access, understand, and integrate. Despite its relative elusiveness, we should be careful not to dismiss it as irrelevant or unimportant, as has too often been done. The truth is that a proper understanding of the inferior function is indispensable in the human quest for wholeness and integration.

As is the case with other types, INTJs display a "love-hate" relationship with their inferior function, Extraverted Sensing (Se). This is especially true for those in Phase II of type development. Fortunately, the challenges associated with the inferior can be largely offset by understanding its essential nature, as well as potential ways of integrating it.

Generally speaking, having Se as their inferior function makes INTJs less attuned to the details or concrete elements of life. While Se takes in plenty of sensory data from the outside world, what INTJs typically experience is an Ni synthesis of that information. So instead of registering particular environmental details (Se), they see the world through the lens of Ni impressions. They can therefore seem rather oblivious to the details of their surroundings.

This is not to say, however, that INTJs are unaffected by, or insensitive to, their physical environment. Although they may be consciously oblivious to their surroundings, they are still absorbing and subconsciously registering a breadth of environmental stimuli.

Similar to INFJs, their nervous systems are often highly permeable and sensitive to the environment. This is why they commonly know things without realizing how they came to know them. They passively absorb information apart from conscious effort. This permeability can also make them susceptible to overstimulation in noisy or chaotic circumstances.

Because of their conscious disconnect from the world around them, many INTJs report feeling like aliens or strangers in the world, even estranged from their own bodies. This can make them leery of unfamiliar S experiences, such as trying new foods, drugs, or physical activities. Doing so can seem too risky or unpredictable, since the S world seems largely outside of INTJs' sphere of control.

In time, however, INTJs may gradually become more open to and interested in S novelties. Those intrigued by their inferior Se may display a surprising thirst for sensory novelty, material comforts, or physical thrills. They may drive expensive cars, purchase luxurious homes, or opt for high-end accommodations when traveling. Some even become connoisseurs of fine food, wine, or art.

This points to the love-hate relationship INTJs often have with their inferior function. Depending on time and circumstances, Se matters may be viewed as a source of great pleasure and intrigue, or one of fear, stress, and frustration.

Mind-Body Disconnect

Not only do INTJs feel disconnected to the physical world around them, but also to their own bodies. In his book, *Jung's Four and Some Philosophers*, Thomas King describes the experience of the INJ type: "His hands are alien to him and his body unfamiliar."

Because of their poor inner bodily perception (a job best handled by Introverted Sensing), INTJs are often plagued by health-related fears, even nightmares, regarding unforeseen assaults on their health. They commonly fear medical procedures of all sorts, perhaps because of deep-seated uncertainty about how that foreign thing called their body might respond.

For similar reasons, INTJs may routinely forget to eat and appear undernourished. Others may overeat because of diminished attention to what, or how much, they are consuming. One of our INJ blog readers described his experience this way:

> *"I regularly forget to eat, or put it off because of the effort it takes to prepare sustenance, or because it may detract from the pleasure of being in my mind . . . I don't like to physically "do" much of anything. It is also very startling for me to be touched without invitation, which seems to jerk me out of my mind and forces me to pay attention to sensation. There are also times I try to grasp my present reality and suddenly feel afraid. I look around and think, "I am in this body . . . in this house . . . with these walls . . . around these people . . . and they are my family . . . who are these people?" Thinking about these things can upset my stomach or may even cause me to hyperventilate. It's not that I don't love my family. It's just when I try to focus on the here and now, it can be pretty terrifying, as if I'm an ancient being suddenly waking up in someone else's body."*

In her piece, "How INJs Approach their Body and Physical Needs," Elaine Schallock observes:

> *"For INJs there is an extreme level of distrust, even demonization, of the body and its processes because S remains so alien and out of their control. Physiological responses are not well understood and often not accurately perceived; even supposedly pleasurable physiological feelings are regularly repressed and/or dismissed as unwanted. So-called "thrill seeking" which brings up butterflies of excitement for other types can be a source of anguish for Ni types who may experience that bodily response as pain, nausea, or dizziness . . ."*

Schallock continues:

> *"Long-term physical suffering is seen as the epitome of the worst kind of evil and the deepest of their fears. If this occurs . . . they may become angry and incredulous, convinced that the body is lashing out against them somehow. Some INJs react by becoming positively punitive, subjecting themselves to even more physical stress by doing things like slamming back a potentially unsafe dose of NSAIDS or exercising to the point of injury. They tend not to react gently or respectfully toward the body, blaming and disciplining when things go awry."*

In trying to compensate for this mind-body disconnect, INTJs may develop and adhere to rather strict regimens of diet, exercise, and/or medical care. Without these types of structures and safeguards in place, they may worry that their mind-body disconnect might somehow precipitate, or render them oblivious to, a potentially serious health crisis.

Impracticality & Subsistence

The inferior nature of their Se also makes INTJs the least practical of the T types. This is partly due to their S obliviousness and partly to their general preference for N over S. Hence, it would not be uncommon to find an INTJ capable of explaining complex laws of physics who, at the same time, seems clueless (or at least highly apathetic) when it comes to filling out his income taxes.

While all types may worry about money and ensuring that their basic S needs are met, subsistence-related fears are typically more prominent among INTJs (and INFJs). Realizing their tenuous relationship to S world, they may frequently worry that something will go awry in their attempts to secure S provisions. Not only are they unsure of their own S competence, but also of the degree to which they can trust the world to be fair and generous with them. To compensate, they may turn to others to help them navigate life's S details. This can help, at least to some extent, to allay their S fears and reassure them that it is safe and okay to stay focused on their N work.

One of the more difficult realities for INTJs is that, in order for their Ni to work optimally, their S needs must first be satisfied to a certain level. This is typically not a problem for INTJs as children, since their S subsistence is supplied by their parents. But once they hit adulthood and are expected to fend for themselves, they are suddenly faced with a more ominous reality. While they would love to earn a living by proffering their N theories or insights to the world, many INTJ adults discover that translating N ideas into S provisions is not as easy or surefire as they anticipated. Those who are fortunate enough to find work that is rewarding on both the N and S fronts may manage to circumvent this problem. But those whose career is either unsatisfying on an N level or fails to pay the bills may feel stuck. They may therefore feel forced to either take a higher-paying, but ultimately less satisfying job, or to continue being plagued by S concerns that impair their N focus or productivity.

Perfectionism

Both INTJs and INFJs are notorious for their predilection for perfectionism. Fortunately, this propensity is well-explained by type theory. Namely, INJs can be understood as striving to integrate their dominant Ni with their inferior Se, to see their N ideals perfectly materialized in S reality.

Parenthetically, while it is true that ENPs also have a dominant N (i.e., Ne) and inferior S (i.e., Si) function, Ne tends not to get attached to a single vision in the way that Ni does. Where Ne is open to multiple interpretations or possibilities, Ni sees only one. So although some ENPs can be perfectionists (Steve Jobs is a good example), perfectionism is a more consistent and signature tendency of INJs.

One of INTJ my friends, for instance, spent well over a month working to resolve a problem with the rendering of bullet points in his business's email newsletters. Despite the fact that the problem would only be noticeable to about 10% of his email clientele, not to mention that it was considered intractable by many email experts, he continued to relentlessly pursue a solution. Ultimately, after many weeks of work and frustration, he managed to find his own workaround.

As suggested by this example, perfectionism, thoroughness, and perseverance (or what some might call obsessiveness or compulsiveness) are closely linked for INTJs. Many feel they cannot rest or move forward until certain foundational matters have been squared away. While other types might content themselves with "good enough," INTJs are insistent that their work meets their own (often very high) standards of excellence. Moreover, INTJs can rarely be convinced by others that their behavior is extreme or irrational. And even if they could be, they may feel incapable of changing it. The compulsion is simply too strong to readily relinquish. Once again, Schallock's insight proves instructive:

> *"Instead of being open to a modification of the plan, INJs hold on ever more tightly to the original vision, feeling as though this is the only way to correct the problem. They are then caught in a paradox. To sacrifice the Ni vision would mean giving up the dominant function, the very center of their "sense of self." They are, understandably, loathed to do so. But ultimately what INJs must realize is that this is an illusion. What is touted as a commitment to the Ni vision is really a veiled commitment to the Se outcome. Of course, the line between Ni and Se is incredibly thin (where does a concept end and the object begin?), which accounts for the ease by which they accidentally fall prey to such illusions."*

Here, Schallock provides a critical nugget of wisdom. Namely, she highlights the distinction between an Ni vision and its Se manifestation, one which is often conflated in the INTJ mind. Put differently, in their quest to marry Ni and Se, INTJs are not only inclined to see themselves as visionaries, but also as responsible for the materialization of their visions. So instead of seeing their role as limited to deep knowing or analysis (Ni-Te), they unwittingly take the extra step and try to control the S effects or outcomes of their vision, a role which is probably better left to other types (e.g., S types).

To deal with this problem, Schallock advises INTJs to focus primarily on seeing and articulating truth (Ni-Te), while resisting the temptation to become overly involved with its application or materialization (Se). In other words, when INTJs stop trying to control or micromanage Se outcomes, they are less apt to be gripped by perfectionism. This may be why many INTJs have found a satisfying home in academics, a setting where they can develop theories more or less independently of their application.

INTJ "Subtypes"

As I touched on earlier, there is a fair amount of intratype variability among INTJs. While all INTJs use the same four functions, some focus on certain functions more than others. To explain these differences, it can be useful to invoke the commonly used "nature-nurture" distinction. I am inclined to believe that nature and nurture play roughly equal roles in shaping personality. So even if we attributed half of INTJs' personality characteristics to their inborn type, there would still be ample room for circumstantial factors to introduce variations and differences, as well as abnormalities.

With that said, I am a typologist, which means I am most interested in exploring "normal" personality patterns (as opposed, for instance, to studying personality disorders). So while it is true that life circumstances may lead some INTJs to develop abnormal characteristics, I see my job as one of describing INTJ variations that fall within the spectrum of normal personality.

Based on my own observations, as well as extant research on INTJs, I propose four primary INTJ subtypes. While many INTJs will identify with one of these subtypes, some may see elements of themselves across two or more of them. This is perfectly okay and not at all surprising, since all of the subtypes are ultimately rooted in the same personality structure that we call INTJ. Moreover, I don't feel it terribly important to identify one's subtype with absolute certainty. My main concern is to demonstrate the range of possibilities that exist within the INTJ type, which will hopefully make it easier for INTJs to correctly identify and understand their type.

Although I discerned the four INTJ subtypes largely through empirical means, they can also be explained rationally. Namely, each can be seen as emphasizing one or two of the INTJ's personality functions over the others. This is not to say that a given subtype will not use, or feel compelled to explore, the other functions. After all, the overarching goal for INTJs is to develop and integrate all four functions. For this reason, it is not uncommon for INTJs to move out of one subtype and into another. In fact, in many cases this signifies growth. So while each of the following subtypes falls within the normal range of INTJ presentations, some can be considered healthier or more developed than others.

It is my conviction that the development and regular employment of the auxiliary function is a critical first step toward integration for all types. It is helpful to think of the auxiliary as a sort of bridge between the dominant and inferior function. Without this bridge, INTJs may see no alternative to making huge, bipolar leaps between their Ni and Se. Doing so results in extreme or unhealthy attitudes and behaviors, including INTJs' Achilles' heel—perfectionism.

With this in mind, our first two subtypes, the "status / power seeker" and the "creative / aesthete," can be viewed as generally less developed or integrated than the "theorist" or "diagnostician" subtypes. In emphasizing neither Ni nor Te, the status / power seeker might be considered the least healthy of the subtypes, whereas both the theorist and diagnostician subtypes routinely use both of these functions, making them most likely to consistently achieve psychological health and integration.

"The Status / Power Seeker" (Se Emphasis)

This subtype emphasizes external rewards and status (Se). This may include striving for fame, power, and/or wealth. This subtype roughly corresponds to the Enneagram types Three and Eight. While not the most common INTJ subtype, it highlights the allure of Se rewards for INTJs.

It is not always easy to discern the driving motivation of a given INTJ, especially from without. Moreover, not all INTJs who become rich or famous are motivated primarily by wealth or egotism. For some, these S rewards are simply by-products of their achievements in a given field. At the same time, there is no *a priori* reason to believe that INTJs are less interested in, or motivated by, ego or inferior-function rewards than other types. Therefore, determining whether a given INTJ falls into this subtype requires discernment and perspicacity.

Some INTJs of this subtype may be drawn to the political sphere. I will leave it up to the reader to decide, for instance, whether INTJs like Hillary Clinton, Al Gore, Henry Kissinger, or former Federal Reserve Chairman, Alan Greenspan, fall into this subtype. Of course, politics is only one of many paths to Se status. INTJs in STEM careers (science, technology, engineering, mathematics), not to mention fields like business, law, or finance, may also enjoy myriad opportunities for achieving power, status, and influence.

This subtype may also be motivated by the prospect of financial security. One can easily see why INTJs might pursue wealth as a means of assuaging their fears of S deprivation. Moreover, many INTJs appreciate high-quality goods such as fine automobiles, art, food/ wine, architecture, etc. So they may not only seek wealth for the sake of financial security, but also as a means of accessing a smorgasbord of modern Se pleasures.

"The Creative / Aesthete" (Ni-Se Emphasis)

Our second INTJ subtype is the "creative / aesthete." In using the term aesthete, I am referring to INTJs with an overriding concern for aesthetic / sensory appreciation or sophistication. We might also use the term connoisseur.

I have known several INTJs of this subtype who are bona fide "foodies." They relish any opportunity to appreciate and evaluate new foods and drinks (Se). Some may even take up work as chefs or sommeliers. Others of this subtype may exhibit affinities for fine art or architecture. I once knew an INTJ attorney who was such a huge art connoisseur that he ran out of wall space to display his full collection. Still other INTJs may display an overriding interest in comedy and satire. As I mentioned earlier, one of my INTJ friends starts his day by visiting 9gag.com to enjoy some early laughs. What all of these INTJs have in common is a strong interest in perception and aesthetic appreciation. Equally important, they do so with relatively little incorporation of their auxiliary Te.

Similar to INFJs, INTJs of this subtype may not only appreciate art, but may also try their hand at creating it (Se). This is attractive to INTJs because it incorporates both their Ni and Se; Ni supplies the vision or idea, while Se is charged with its materialization. This provides INTJs with at least some sense of dominant-inferior integration, as both functions work toward a common goal. I am inclined to count author Stephen King, comedian George Carlin, and creator of the Dilbert comic strip, Scott Adams, among INTJs of this subtype.

Elaine Schallock has been fairly critical of INTJs (and INFJs) of this subtype. She sees this subtype as combining Ni and Se in a way that mimics Ne, or what she has pejoratively called "bastardized Ne." According to Schallock, Ni is characteristically a convergent function and is best used to understand and describe "what is." She sees Ne, by contrast, as a divergent and creative function, making it better suited to artistic enterprises. Therefore, Schallock suggests that INTJs' Ni is better partnered with Te for the sake of analysis, rather than trying to directly materialize Ni ideals through Se. I should probably mention that Schallock levels a similar criticism toward NPs who forsake their divergent role in favor of trying to operate convergently (i.e., "bastardized Ni").

With that said, Schallock does go a bit easier on INTJs working creatively with words or ideas (i.e., with N things) than she does on those functioning as visual artists or performers (i.e., S activities). In her view, the latter group must spend an inordinate amount of time and energy developing their weakest function (Se), which requires putting their type's greatest strength—convergent N knowing—on the proverbial backburner.

We might also grant an added measure of grace to INTJs pursuing engineering or architecture. While these fields in many respects encourage INTJs to function like Ne types, the heavy demands they place on N and T make them preferable to F-centric creative enterprises.

In closing our discussion of this subtype, one could argue that it is spurious to suggest that INTJ creatives such as Stephen King, George Carlin, or Scott Adams were somehow mistaken in their vocational choices. After all, each left his own indelible, creative mark on the world. At the same time, one could maintain that these individuals may have been equally, perhaps even more, successful had they pursued analytic or scientific types of work. But we cannot discount the deep importance of motivation. Even if most INTJs are best off performing analytic or investigative work, there will always be those who are irrevocably drawn to a certain art form. In such cases, it is probably futile, perhaps even misguided, to try to persuade them otherwise. If they are ultimately meant to do something else, time, circumstance, and intuition will likely be their best teachers.

"The Theorist" (Ni-Te or Ni-Fi Emphasis)

The purpose of Ni is to apprehend deep structural truths or causal patterns. While Ne types may explore and experiment with a smattering of theories, Ni works more convergently, proffering a singular theory or framework based on available data. This is why Schallock sees working with theories as an excellent vocation for INJs, allowing them to routinely use Ni as it was intended.

We can divide INTJ theorists into two groups: those emphasizing Ni-Te and those emphasizing Ni-Fi. The former often performs theoretical work in STEM fields, developing scientific, mathematical, or computational theories. They enjoy studying the structures and patterns of physical systems. Examples include INTJs like Stephen Hawking and John Nash. For those familiar with the Enneagram, such thinkers would be classified as Fives with a Six wing (5w6).

Those in the Ni-Fi camp are more psychologically minded. Many take interest in abnormal psychology, such as the study of psychopathy or various personality disorders. As mentioned in our section on Fi, they may enjoy exploring the effects of past abuse or trauma on the psyche (e.g., childhood "wounds"). In this respect, their interests may overlap with those of NFPs. INTJs in this camp often test as type 5w4 on the Enneagram.

INTJs may also enjoy theoretical work in the field of philosophy. Those with a stronger Te bent often gravitate toward "analytic philosophy," which resembles science in its concern for control and precision. Philosophers with stronger Fi interests, such as French philosopher Jean Paul Sartre, may function more like the creative /

aesthetic subtype. Sartre, for instance, wrote several novels, which is typically not the preferred mode of expression for INTJs with stronger Te. I would place the INTJ writer Daniel Quinn, best known for his thought-provoking novel, Ishmael, in a similar category as Sartre. While it has been difficult for me to know with confidence whether Nietzsche was an INTJ or INFJ, his philosophical works also exemplify Ni in combination with Feeling.

While Ni-Te theorizing is undoubtedly one of the healthiest roles for INTJs, even those in the Ni-Fi camp can be seen as more developed than some of the other subtypes. At minimum, routine employment of Fi helps INTJs counterbalance Perceiving with regular doses of Judging.

"The Diagnostician" (Ni-Te or Ni-Fi Emphasis)

It is common to associate the act of diagnosis with medical practice. But in discussing this subtype, I am connoting something much broader than that. Namely, a diagnosis is really just an analysis of the nature and causes of a given phenomenon. This of course has similarities to the work performed by INTJ theorists. The primary difference is that diagnosticians are more practical in their focus. They don't engage in analysis for its own sake, but have practical reasons for doing so. Most typically, this involves finding solutions to specific problems.

As we saw with INTJ theorists, the diagnostician subtype can be divided into Ni-Te and Ni-Fi camps. A good example of the former is Dr. Gregory House, the featured character of the popular television show, *House*. If you've ever seen the show, you're well aware of the fact that Dr. House exhibits an almost absurdly poor bedside manner, showing little in the way of sensitivity to his patients' feelings, nor those of his colleagues. But whatever House lacks in bedside manner is more than made up for in his skill as a diagnostician. His ability to think differently from his colleagues (i.e., to wield Ni) allows him to routinely identify the correct diagnosis with far greater speed and precision.

Former vice president Al Gore is another good example of this subtype. This is evidenced in Gore's growing number of penetrating books on subjects like politics, the environment, and economics. Few thinkers have more knowledge or understanding of the big picture than Gore. This has allowed him to accurately diagnose and proffer potential solutions for some of the world's most pressing problems.

INTJ diagnosticians with an Ni-Fi bent may be drawn to working as psychologists, psychiatrists, life coaches, and the like. They enjoy using their knowledge of psychology, as well as the specific information they collect from their clients, to identify problems and therapeutic solutions. Like INFJs, they believe that a proper understanding of a problem is the most important step in its amelioration. Hence, such INTJs often see their primary role as one of enlightening others about the deeper psychological sources of their attitudes, motivations, and behavior.

Schallock sees the diagnostic role, especially when Ni-Te centered, as another great use of INTJs' signature strengths. It allows Ni to do what it does best—to assess a problem and discern its underlying causes and structure.

INTP

INTPs make up about 3-4% of the general population. Their dominant function is Introverted Thinking (Ti), which can be associated with high levels of focus, self-discipline, intentionality, independence, and intensity of thought. Such are the INTP's signature strengths.

Although INTPs may not discover their intellectual side (i.e., their N) as early as INTJs do, once their auxiliary Ne is fully awakened, they take intellectual matters very seriously. They work to discern unifying themes and metaphysical truths that explain the underlying nature of things. Especially early in their intellectual journey, they feel they must develop a sufficient understanding of the whole before they can competently assess any of its constituent parts. Toward this end, INTPs may devour stacks of books on subjects like philosophy, religion, psychology, and evolutionary theory.

When vacationing from their personal projects and investigations, INTPs can be quirky, witty, and engaging. Since they extravert Intuition (Ne) and Feeling (Fe), they can have a certain charm, approachability, and congeniality about them. When discussing a topic that interests them, they can be stimulating conversationalists, as their ever active minds can easily connect one topic to another, paving the way for a multifaceted and broad-ranging dialogue. If disinterested however, such as when forced to endure protracted small talk, they will quickly zone out or find a way of redirecting the conversation.

Despite appearing outwardly genuine and personable, INTPs are more interested in discussing ideas than the commonplace details of people's lives. They enjoy discovering what makes people tick—their motivations, interests, patterns, and propensities. This allows INTPs to further hone and refine their theories (Ti-Ne) of human nature (Fe).

Like other introverts, INTPs can be anxious and self-conscious characters. It is not uncommon for them to display a handful of nervous habits, or at least some sign that they are not at ease. They generally avoid direct eye contact, as though the gaze of their interlocutor may somehow harm them or render them incapable of thinking or communicating. INTPs often have enough insecurity about the discombobulated nature of their Ne expressions in the first place. Feeling that someone else is watching or critiquing them only makes it worse.

INTPs can also be slow to disclose the contents of their inner world. As strange as it may seem to extraverts, INTPs often conceal some of their most dominant personality features, namely, their highly cerebral, rational side. It may only be a select few who are granted full access to this side of the INTP. Others may only encounter INTPs' inner world through encounters with their work, such as by reading something they have written. This may explain why many INTPs often take interest in writing, which provides an excellent forum for expressing themselves more fully and precisely.

Because of their reluctance to freely display the rational dimension of their personality, as well as the scattered nature of their Ne expressions, INTPs often feel their true level of knowledge and competence goes unnoticed by others. This is especially common in the workplace, where their lack of enthusiasm for organizational life, combined with their quirky outward demeanor, may be mistaken for incompetence.

INTPs' Functional Stack & Type Development

INTPs' functional stack is composed of the following functions:

Dominant: Introverted Thinking (Ti)

Auxiliary: Extraverted Intuition (Ne)

Tertiary: Introverted Sensing (Si)

Inferior: Extraverted Feeling (Fe)

INTPs' personality type development can be broadly conceived as consisting of three phases:

Phase I (Childhood)

This phase is characterized by the emergence and differentiation of INTPs' dominant function, Introverted Thinking (Ti). Early in life, INTPs often employ their Ti to focus on one or two pursuits. They may, for instance, use it to master video games, program computers, get good grades, or perfect their 5-K time. Since Ti is a Judging function, INTPs tend to take themselves and their lives quite seriously. Even from a relatively young age, they are self-disciplined and goal-oriented, striving for excellence in whatever captures their interests.

Phase II (Adolescence-30s)

Once their dominant Ti reaches a certain level of consciousness and differentiation, INTPs' inferior function, Extraverted Feeling (Fe), enters the picture and begins to play a more influential role. INTPs are not immune from the dominant-inferior wrestlings described in our Introduction, making this phase as challenging for them as it is for other types.

Phase II INTPs also show increasing use and development of their auxiliary function, Extraverted Intuition (this can also begin in

Phase I for some INTPs). During this phase, INTPs often develop a stronger interest in intellectual and philosophical endeavors, poised to see and understand "the big picture." They also become more skeptical toward certain Ti conclusions they made in Phase I. Developing their Ne involves an opening of prior judgments to allow an influx of new information. But since Ne is extraverted and expansive, INTPs must explore a breadth of ideas before they feel confident about who they are and what they believe. Thus, Phase II INTPs may find it much easier to identify what they *don't* believe than what they do believe. Many will struggle with nihilism and relativism, worried that they may never find absolute truth. It can therefore take INTPs a great deal of time, even well into their thirties, to discern what they believe about the world and about themselves, let alone figure out what they should be doing. Unfortunately, societal pressures and expectations often push Phase II INTPs (as well as other types) into relationships or careers well before they are ready.

Phase II INTPs may also begin to tap into their tertiary function, Introverted Sensing (Si). They use their Si to recall past experiences and acquired wisdom. This prevents them from having to retread paths they have already explored in the past.

Phase III (30s, 40s, & Beyond)

If all goes well and they are fortunate enough to enter Phase III, INTPs become increasingly aware of the insidious ways of their inferior Fe. As they become more aware of their inferior and learn to function more authentically as INTPs, they experience greater balance between their Ti and Fe. They learn that integrating their Fe happens naturally and indirectly as they go about authentically using their Ti and Ne. As they cultivate conditions that support their natural strengths, Phase III INTPs come to experience a heightened sense of peace, wholeness, and satisfaction.

INTPs' Dominant Function: Introverted Thinking (Ti)

To understand INTPs, or other IP types, it is necessary to recognize the full implications of their dominant function, Ti, being a Judging function. Namely, INTPs are best understood as predominant Judgers and display many characteristics of EJs, only that these behaviors are directed inwardly or toward the self.

Ti involves the application of logic and reason for the sake of understanding a given situation, system, or problem. INTPs use Ti to bring structure and order to their inner world, granting them a strong sense of inner control. Inwardly, INTPs are highly self-disciplined, working to effectively manage their thoughts and their lives. The disciplined nature of their Ti compels INTPs to frame many things as a goal or challenge. These challenges may be physical (e.g., trying to achieve an ideal state of health or fitness), intellectual, practical, psychoemotional (e.g., becoming self-actualized), or later in their development, interpersonal (e.g., "perfecting" a relationship or becoming a skilled lover). In order to succeed in these personal challenges, INTPs are apt to impose rules on themselves. However, because of the wayward influence of their auxiliary Ne, they commonly end up breaking or sabotaging them.

INTPs are also less interested in working with facts than with ideas. Jung writes: "His ideas have their origin not in objective data, but in his subjective foundation." INTPs are constantly digging into the background of their own thoughts in order to better understand their origins and to ensure their thinking is founded on solid reasoning. They see it pointless to try to build theories on a dubious conceptual platform, making them slower than Te types to rush into experiments to discover more "facts."

INTPs often find it easier to identify inconsistencies or logical shortcomings—to assert what is *not* true—than to identify and confidently assert what *is* true. They can quickly locate inconsistencies or logical shortcomings in a given theory or argument. They excel when it comes to identifying exceptions or imagining scenarios in which the proposed explanation could breakdown. Due to their sensitivity to theoretical exceptions, they can be quick to throw theories and start from scratch. INTJs, by contrast, seem less deterred by ostensible exceptions, perhaps feeling that they will eventually be explained or otherwise rectified.

When functioning constructively, INTPs, like INFPs, often employ a trial-and-error sort of approach to building their theories and ideas. INTPs start with a given (Ti) and then use their auxiliary Ne to explore various connections and possibilities. They also integrate past experiences and acquired knowledge through their tertiary Si. It is usually only after years of toying with ideas that something resembling a systematic and coherent theory may start to emerge.

We can also compare and contrast Ti with Fi. IFPs generally take up moral, artistic, personal, or humanitarian concerns (Fi) before logical or intellectual ones (Ti). They judge in terms of good and bad, love and hate, like and dislike. Conversely, for INTPs, things must first pass the test of reason. They think less in terms of like and dislike than they do of likely and unlikely, logical and illogical. This is why INTPs generally prefer working with ideas and concepts rather than more subjective, taste-oriented matters like the arts.

INTPs' Auxiliary Function: Extraverted Intuition (Ne)

INTPs use Extraverted Intuition (Ne) as their auxiliary function. Ne can function either perceptively or expressively. The verbal expression of Ne amounts to something like brainstorming aloud. When orating, INTPs may not always seem to "have a point" as they haphazardly drift from one idea to the next. Even ideas that seem inwardly logical and sensible INTPs may suddenly sound incoherent when they attempt to convey them through their Ne.

In its receptive role, Ne prompts INTPs to gather information. Ne does not merely gather sensory information as Se does. Rather, it goes beyond or looks behind sense data, allowing INTPs to discern otherwise hidden patterns, possibilities, and potentials. Their Ne is constantly scanning for relationships or patterns within a pool of facts, ideas or experiences. INTPs commonly use this receptive side of their Ne in activities such as reading, researching, and conversation. They enjoy asking questions that allow them to gain insight or knowledge from others, making INTPs good facilitators of conversation.

INTPs may also use their Ne to sniff out intriguing possibilities. They commonly enjoy and assume the role of wanderer or seeker, rarely knowing in advance exactly what they are seeking.

Ne also confers open-mindedness, helping INTPs see truth on both sides of an issue without forming unwarranted judgments or premature conclusions. More specifically, their Ne can be seen as contributing to their openness to alternative or Bohemian lifestyles. INTPs are those most likely to suddenly become vegetarians, join a commune, or decide to live out of the back of a van. They are drawn to the idea and challenges of an unconventional lifestyle.

Like other NPs, INTPs often have a love-hate relationship with their Ne. They love the fact that it helps them remain open-minded and grasp the bigger picture. But living with Ne also has its challenges. For one, it can make it difficult for INTPs to arrive at firm conclusions or make important decisions. It often seems that at the very moment they are feeling good about a given conclusion or decision, their Ne steps in and causes them to start doubting it again. This has obvious implications for INTPs who are trying to find their niche in the world. This can leave them feeling discouraged and restless, worried that they may never find what they are looking for. They may feel frustrated by their seeming lack of progress toward anything substantial. The fact is that INTPs desperately want to produce something of lasting worth or value, but they also want to ensure they get it right. They don't want to leave any stone unturned before arriving at a conclusion. While INTPs typically enjoy this quest for truth, there comes a point when they begin to feel the pressures of life impinging on them. Questions about careers and relationships loom large as they enter their late twenties and thirties. This can be frustrated to INTPs as they feel like life is requiring them to make decisions long before they are ready. As is true of all IN types, they feel that life would be better if they weren't forced to reckon with practical concerns.

INTPs' Tertiary Function: Introverted Sensing (Si)

Unlike Ne (or Se), INTPs' tertiary function, Introverted Sensing (Si), is a conservative function. It involves an attachment to past experiences and past precedent—to the routine, familiar, and predictable. Types with Si in their functional stack, including INTPs, tend to eat a fairly routine or consistent diet, "eating to live" rather than "living to eat." Si types are not only conservative with regard to their diet, but with respect to the material world in general. They tend to be savers rather than spenders, seeing excessive material consumption as unnecessary, or perhaps even immoral.

Like other Si types, INTPs also have a diminished need for novel physical pleasures, lavish surroundings, or material comforts. They are minimalists to the core, relatively unconcerned with their physical surroundings.

An often overlooked role of Si is its perception of internal bodily sensations—the body as felt and experienced from within. Perhaps more than any other function, it provides access to the raw and basic sense of "being" that exists apart from thought or outward stimuli. Historically, Eastern philosophical and religious traditions have done a much better job exploring this dimension than those of the West. This feature of Si is brought to the fore during activities requiring close attention to one's internal bodily state, such as yoga, Tai-Chi, meditation, or various relaxation techniques. INTPs interested in exploring this element of Si may find great delight and benefit from these sorts of practices. They are especially useful in developing the body awareness necessary to relax and control anxiety.

INTPs' Fourth/Inferior Function: Extraverted Feeling (Fe)

As enumerated in my recent book, The INTP, INTPs can be easily blinded to the degree to which their inferior function impacts their decisions and behavior. In order to avoid being subconsciously controlled and unduly influenced by their Fe, INTPs can benefit from understanding Fe in general, as well as the ways it tends to manifest in their own personality type.

Harmony vs. Helping

Since Fe is INTPs' inferior function, it is often more sensitive and less resilient than it is in FJ types. This can make INTPs extremely uncomfortable in emotional situations, especially those involving potential conflict or disharmony.

Because of their Fe's concern for maintaining external harmony (or what may be better understood as its discomfort with disharmony), INTPs may abstain from expressing their judgments in order to avoid unsettling others. While not as overtly warm or effusive as FJ types, INTPs can be sensitive to others' feelings and may go out of their way to avoid hurting or offending them. For instance, in the midst of a discussion, an INTP may want to explain how human mating practices are primarily a product of evolutionary pressures. But if she suspects that others may take offense to such an explanation, she may withhold it to avoid introducing disharmony.

Although functioning as superficial peacemakers, INTPs are generally slower to go out of their way to help others (at least in direct, hands-on ways). Especially early in their development, most forgo community service and avoid investing extensive time and energy helping others. This is particularly evident when under stress. If burdened by too many external pressures or demands, INTPs' willingness to help others is one of the first things to go.

In short, INTPs' Fe is more concerned with preserving harmony than it is with extensive helping. This is especially true early in life, when they have yet to achieve their Ti goals. Once those goals have been satisfactorily met, however, they may become more benevolent. We can see this with Einstein, for instance, who displayed increasing beneficence and generosity toward people in the second half of his life.

Reluctance to Extravert Judgment

Unlike J-types, INTPs are uncomfortable issuing orders and directives. This is why, whenever possible, they shy away from leadership roles. For the same reason, parenting and disciplining children can be challenging for INTPs.

We've already discussed one reason why INTPs are slow to extravert judgment—their fear of disharmony. But there are other reasons as well. One is that Ne is the first extraverted function in their functional stack. So instead of directly expressing a judgment, they may do so in less direct ways, such as through hints or questions (e.g., "Are you sure you want to do that?").

They may also refrain from expressing judgments because they have yet to settle an issue in their own minds. INTPs never want to be seen as dogmatic, closed-minded, or unnuanced in their thinking. Relatedly, they are naturally slow to advise others, especially with regard to F-related matters. This is because INTPs don't want to get it wrong, to deal with the aftermath of being wrong, or to make decisions that involve or affect other people.

INTPs may also avoid extraverting their judgments because of concerns about their ability to effectively articulate them, fearing that this may cause them to be perceived as less intelligent than they really are.

Considering these and other hesitations, it can require a fair amount of courage for INTPs to assert themselves, particularly when discussing controversial or otherwise uncomfortable issues. INTJs, in contrast, whose extraverted Judging function (Te) is in the auxiliary position, seem to have little problem in this regard.

Because of their difficulty with direct self-expression, INTPs are prone to making sudden executive decisions without any prior communication. In such instances, others may be left feeling incredulous as to why the INTP had not thought to discuss the issue with them first. INTPs may also exhibit passive-aggressive forms of behavior, such as intentionally staying late at the office to eschew or resist domestic expectations. They can resemble other IP types in this regard, who have a similar propensity for acting passive-aggressively rather than expressing their concerns more directly.

Convergent Truth & Enlightening Others

As I've written elsewhere, the inferior function can be understood to represent the ultimate goal or attractor point of the personal growth. It is what motivates and draws us forward. For INTPs, this attractor point is the promise of convergent truth; Fe, the final function of their stack, represents this place of convergent truth. They may dream of finding ultimate answers, an ideal career, or the perfect relationship.

Like FJs, INTPs fancy the idea of enlightening others regarding how they might live better lives (Fe). But as we've seen, INTPs can struggle when it comes to directly expressing their judgments. They are more comfortable dialoguing about ideas by way of their auxiliary Ne than delivering Fe advice or declarations.

INTPs can also become impatient with those who are slow to understand or embrace their ideas. They often expect others to learn as quickly and independently as they do. They therefore tend to have mixed feelings when it comes to teaching or counseling others.

Desire for Affirmation/Validation

Fe involves making connections between one's own emotions and those of others. When a successful connection occurs, it results in a sense of validation, of being valued and understood. While INTPs can do a fair job at reading others' emotions and are cognitively aware of the appropriate social response, they often do not "feel" what others are feeling. Despite this difficulty in connecting with others on a feeling level, their Fe still desires the same sense of affirmation and validation that FJs readily receive when engaging with people. This need for affirmation can be seen as a motivating force behind INTPs' desire for achievement. It is why many INTPs score high as Enneagram Threes and display certain narcissistic tendencies. Personally, I never understood my desire to write for a popular audience (rather than an academic one) until I recognized that my Fe was pushing for widespread affirmation.

Because INTPs, wittingly or not, rely on others for affirmation, they may often feel they cannot live without at least one other person in their lives. At other times, they can feel incredibly independent (Ti). Especially when their work is going well, they may feel they don't really need other people. If they manage to completely isolate themselves from others, they will soon begin to feel that something important is missing from their lives. This prompts them to reinitiate contact with others, at least until they feel compelled to assert their independence again. This cycle of alternating between needing and devaluing others is common among INTPs and narcissists alike.

Slippery, All-or-None Emotions

Despite the inferior position of their Fe, INTPs are not emotionless robots. Rather, as is typically the case with the inferior, there is an all-or-nothing character to their Fe. INTPs' emotions seem to have a mind of their own, coming and going as they please. Consequently, INTPs often feel awkward or inept in emotional situations, knowing that they cannot readily summon the situationally-appropriate emotions.

As mentioned previously, INTPs are usually cognitively aware of which emotions are appropriate for a given situation, but without experiencing them directly, they can sound clumsy or mechanical in their expressions. This can be difficult for their romantic partners, particularly for FJ types, since FJs desire a sense of authentic emotional communion. While INTPs may experience strong feelings for their partners while away from them, they may not experience those emotions or may have trouble communicating them while together.

For most INTPs, their Fe is rather naive and childlike. They may, for instance, be easily moved by cheesy romantic comedies or sappy love songs, anything that unconsciously incites their Fe emotions. This can also make INTPs easy targets for love-at-first-sight sorts of infatuation. They are particularly susceptible to being wooed by Feeling types, who can bypass their typical channels of logic and directly appeal to INTPs' less conscious Fe.

While INTPs struggle to directly summon or contact their emotions, they can readily override or detach from them, almost functioning as though they didn't exist. Consequently, INTPs may not consciously struggle with the same degree of guilt, regret, or shame as other types. Others may be surprised how quickly INTPs can seemingly resume "business as usual" after what most would consider tragic or traumatic circumstances.

ISTP

ISTP is another of our 16 personality types. While some estimates suggest ISTPs comprise only 5% of the general population, my research and experience suggests this type to be more common. Male ISTPs are thought to outnumber ISTP females at a clip of three to one.

Like INTPs, ISTPs dominant function is Introverted Thinking (Ti), which can be associated with high levels of focus, self-discipline, intentionality, independence, and intensity of thought. ISTPs take life rather seriously and use their inner logic to discern the best ways of navigating it. They may, for instance, use Ti to work out their own personal methods for maximizing performance in a particular sport. They love using their Ti to solve practical problems or to optimize functioning. Because of their independence, self-directedness, and competitiveness, ISTPs may excel at nearly anything they set their mind to.

Because ISTPs' Thinking is introverted in its direction (Ti), it often goes unnoticed by outsiders. What others tend to see is ISTPs' engaging in action (Se) or mixing with people (Fe). ISTPs' Extraverted Feeling (Fe) can bring a surprising amount of affability and personableness to their outward presentation. ISTPs often present as sincere, genuine, and approachable. Their Fe confers a certain childlike innocence that others may find refreshing.

Since neither Ti nor Se is a highly verbal function, ISTPs can be persons of few words. Their relationships are often built around shared interests or activities rather than extensive conversation. But since status and reputation are important to their Se and Fe, ISTPs may be far more talkative at work or in public settings than they are at home. In public, they may be fun and outgoing. In private, they may seem more aloof or disengaged, sensing that their intimates cannot provide them the same degree of ego boost they find in the public arena (Fe). This ostensible disparity between their private and public persona may lead their intimates to consider them narcissistic or hypocritical.

ISTPs commonly display conventional, sometimes stylish, forms of dress. While their Ti is concerned with functionality and practicality, their Se and Fe are attuned to the trendy and popular. Physically, ISTPs may have either a lanky or muscular build. While athletic engagement often keeps them fit throughout their childhood, their love for food (Se) may lead to problems with weight in adulthood.

While not to the same extent as their ESTP counterparts, ISTPs are undeterred from investing in high quality and/or high-status goods. Like other Se types, they can appreciate excellent food (some are even foodies) and stylish clothing. Their Ti "techiness" also lends an interest to top-notch technology or equipment. Fancy or vintage sports cars, motorcycles, or power tools commonly line the garages of ISTPs.

Like other SP types, ISTPs often display great kinesthetic intelligence. They are often athletic, mechanically-inclined, and endowed with excellent dexterity and hand-eye coordination. In contrast to INTPs, who sport high levels of mental energy, ISTPs exhibit high levels of physical energy and stamina. While INTPs use their Ne to explore ideas, ISTPs use their hands, body, and other senses to explore and manipulate the concrete world (Se).

Because of their preference for hands-on activities, ISTPs may underperform in academic settings. This is typically not due to a lack of ability *per se*, but a lack of interest or stimulation. As is true for all Sensing types, being forced to deal in abstractions for too long can be draining for ISTPs. Their need for physical activity and impatience with abstractions may also explain why ISTP school children are more likely to be diagnosed with ADD or ADHD than some of the other personality types. ISTP students who can set their focus on a particular career goal or endpoint, such as becoming a surgeon, are apt to fare better.

Generally speaking, ISTPs are wise to pursue careers that allow them to use their practical intelligence to solve concrete problems (i.e., Holland "Realistic" careers). They can make excellent artisans, athletes, mechanics, drummers, maintenance workers, chiropractors, surgeons, pilots, chefs, etc.

While ISTP differ from ISTJs by only one "preference" (i.e., J-P), these types actually share *zero* functions in common. This makes them far more different than is sometimes recognized. As TJ types, ISTJs are more direct and firm (even blunt) in their assertions than ISTPs are. ISTPs use Fe rather than Te, which confers a certain social ease, even charm, which ISTJs often lack. Moreover, ISTPs use Se rather than Si, making them less concerned with preserving past precedent than ISTJs are. Finally, ISTPs are more inclined toward "hands-on" and Realistic careers, whereas ISTJs gravitate toward "white collar" sorts of work.

ISTPs' Functional Stack & Type Development

ISTPs' functional stack is composed of the following functions:

Dominant: Introverted Thinking (Ti)

Auxiliary: Extraverted Sensing (Se)

Tertiary: Introverted Intuition (Ni)

Inferior: Extraverted Feeling (Fe)

ISTPs' personality type development can be broadly conceived as consisting of three phases:

Phase I (Childhood)

This phase is characterized by the emergence and differentiation of ISTPs' dominant function, Introverted Thinking (Ti). Early in life, ISTPs often use their Ti to focus on one or two pursuits. They may for instance, funnel their Ti energies into mastering video games, tinkering with computers, or learning the best way of shooting a basketball. Since they often apply their Ti to hands-on activities—sports, Legos, drumming, video games, and the like—Phase I ISTPs may also show significant development of their auxiliary function, Extraverted Sensing (Se).

Since their Ti is a rational Judging function, ISTPs tend to approach life fairly seriously. Even from a relatively young age, they can be self-disciplined and goal-oriented, striving for excellence in whatever they do. They can differ markedly from ESTPs in this regard, whose dominant function (Se) is a Perceiving function, leading Phase I ESTPs to be more open-ended and easygoing. While both types utilize Se and Ti, ESTPs are more concerned with perceiving or experiencing the outside world (Se), while ISTPs are more intentional, focused, and self-directed (Ti).

Phase II (Adolescence-30s)

Once their dominant Ti reaches a certain level of differentiation, ISTPs' inferior function, Extraverted Feeling (Fe), enters the picture and begins to play a more influential role. We will further explore the effects of ISTPs' Fe later in this profile.

Phase II ISTPs also show increasing use and development of their auxiliary function, Extraverted Sensing (Se). This may involve exploring new hobbies and interests, such as gourmet cooking. As a

Perceiving function, Se also leads to an *opening* of their Ti judgments to see if they pass the test of lived experience. Since Se is an extraverted and expansive function, Phase II ISTPs may feel it necessary to explore a wide range of experiences before arriving at confident conclusions.

Phase II ISTPs may also begin to tap into their tertiary function, Introverted Intuition (Ni), which can subconsciously assist ISTPs in piecing together their Se experiences, further clarifying their identity and worldview.

Phase III (30s, 40s, & Beyond)

If all goes well and they are fortunate enough to enter Phase III, ISTPs become increasingly aware of the insidious ways of their inferior Fe. As they become more aware of their inferior and learn to function more authentically as ISTPs, they experience greater balance between their Ti and Fe. They learn that integrating their Fe happens naturally and indirectly as they go about authentically using their Ti and Se. As they cultivate conditions that support their natural strengths, Phase III ISTPs come to experience a heightened sense of peace, wholeness, and satisfaction.

ISTPs' Dominant Function: Introverted Thinking (Ti)

To understand ISTPs, or other IP types, it is necessary to recognize the full implications of their dominant function, Ti, being a Judging function. Namely, ISTPs are best understood as predominant Judgers and display many characteristics of EJs, only that these behaviors are directed inwardly or toward the self.

Ti involves the use of logic and reason for the sake of understanding a given problem, situation, or system. ISTPs use Ti to solve problems, to optimize functioning, and to bring structure and order to their inner world. This inner structuring grants them a strong sense of inner control. It allows ISTPs to be inwardly self-disciplined and to independently manage their lives and personal projects.

The disciplined nature of Ti may inspire ISTPs to frame their lives in terms of personal challenges or a series of independent projects. While not shying away from competing with others, ISTPs enjoy taking on challenges and projects for the mere pleasure of it. Such challenges may be physical (e.g., trying to achieve an optimal level of fitness), practical (e.g., fixing a car), creative (e.g., craftsmanship), or interpersonal.

At times, the inwardly focused and intentional nature of Ti lead can lead ISTPs to mistype themselves as ISTJs. In so doing, they rightly recognize their inner Judging nature, but wrongly conclude that they must be a J-type. They fail to recognize that the J-P label refers only to *outward* demeanor and behavior. This may partly explain what I see as the under-representation of ISTPs in demographic data.

Ti might also be viewed in terms of *fluid intelligence*, whereas Extraverted Thinking (Te) seems more related to *crystallized intelligence*. Ti is more intuitive, contextual, and right-brained, whereas Te is more procedure-oriented and left-brained. The fluid nature of their Ti, combined with the keen observational powers of their Se, contributes to ISTPs' acumen as practical problem solvers. ISTPs can analyze a situation, discern how things should work, and then determine how to fix it. While a Te type might feel compelled to use schematics or manuals to diagnose the problem, ISTPs rely on their Ti's ability to reason their way through concrete problems, even those they've never encountered. This contributes to their skill as mechanics, maintenance workers, machinists, surgeons, technicians, etc.

ISTPs' Auxiliary Function: Extraverted Sensing (Se)

Introverted Sensing (Si) is conservative with respect to new sensations and the material world. Extraverted Sensing (Se), by contrast, is more materially liberal and novelty-oriented. Se types (especially ESPs) often exhibit a laissez-faire, "eat, drink, and be merry" approach to life.

Unlike Si, Se is not content with routine and familiar experiences. For this reason, ISTPs enjoy physical thrills and new sensations. Their Ti penchant for challenges, combined with the thrill-seeking nature of their Se, makes ISTPs prime candidates for all varieties of extreme/ adventure sports. They may take up rock climbing, sky diving, motocross racing, etc. ISTPs also enjoy team sports, long-distance running, and cycling. Any activity that allows them to see new sights, embrace new challenges, and spring into action is generally welcomed by ISTPs.

Se also attunes to the concrete details and sensory information of the environment by way of the five senses. SP types scan the environment for interesting sensory novelties, noticing details in the environment that other types might readily gloss over. This is why SPs (especially ESPs) often have strong visual recall, or what is sometimes dubbed a "photographic" memory. ISTPs may utilize their Se's attention to detail in any number of ways.

One of my ISTP friends, for instance, enjoys scavenging fields for arrowheads. As he saunters about, his Se scans the environment in hopes of finding another lost treasure. After locating an arrowhead, he further enlists his Se to explore its shape, texture, and other features.

ISTPs also employ their Se in their daily work as mechanics, technicians, chefs, construction workers, etc. They make excellent craftsmen, using their Se to attend to the finest physical details. They love working with their hands and using tools to produce high quality pieces.

Unlike the Ne-Si function pair, which encourages makeshift tool use (Ne) in the name of material conservation (Si), the Se-Ni function pair impels ISTPs to acquire the right tools in order to do the job the "right way." In this vein, ISTPs are not opposed to spending a little extra on high quality tools, parts, etc.

Se also differs from Ne in that it is not a highly verbal or abstract function. So while INTPs enjoy sitting around discussing ideas, ISTPs would often prefer to be "doing" something. Even watching sports can be more stimulating than conversation for ISTPs, since it stimulates their Se and allows them to vicariously participate in the action.

ISTPs' Tertiary Function: Introverted Intuition (Ni)

ISTPs' tertiary function is Introverted Intuition (Ni). In combination with their dominant Ti, ISTPs may display some degree of interest in abstract or theoretical topics. After all, Ni and Ti are the same two introverted functions employed by INFJs, who are among the most theoretical-minded of all types. However, because ISTPs' Ni is more unconscious, it is less accessible to them for immediate intuitive perception. Therefore, like other SP types, ISTPs are more likely to gain insight through analyzing a breadth of life experiences (Ti-Se). Ni can also aid in the process, helping ISTPs synthesize and extract meaning from a breadth of Se experiences.

ISTPs' Inferior Function: Extraverted Feeling (Fe)

Like other types, ISTPs can be blinded to the degree to which their inferior function impacts their decisions and behavior. Without sufficiently understanding the inferior function, Extraverted Feeling (Fe), ISTPs will continue to feel incomplete and be prone to unhealthy decision-making in their careers, lifestyle, and relationships.

The ISTP's personality type dynamics can be largely understood as an attempt find a balance between Ti and Fe, independence (Ti) and interdependence (Fe), self (Ti) and others (Fe). Since Ti and Fe comprise a functional whole, ISTPs intuitively realize that they need to better integrate their Fe in order to feel more whole and complete.

Obsessiveness/Workaholism

"In the grip" of the inferior function, all personality types are prone to acting compulsively and obsessively. Grip experiences can be difficult to escape, since the less conscious self (i.e., the inferior function) takes over as the driver of the personality. While the content of grip experiences may differ across the types, their basic shape is essentially the same.

For ISTPs (and INTPs), being in the grip often involves workaholism. As T dominants, work (including personal projects and hobbies), comprises a central component of ISTPs' identity. In doing what they enjoy, ISTPs are naturally very disciplined and thorough. When they are in the grip, however, they become obsessive, perfectionistic, and unable to let go of whatever they are doing. During such times, ISTPs may alienate themselves from others, insisting they need more and more time to themselves (this is why ISTPs often test as Enneagram Fives). They become trapped, functioning only in Judging mode (Ti-Fe), while forgoing the Perceiving functions (Se-Ni) in the middle of their functional stack.

As for all types, the process of slipping into grip experiences is often subtle and insidious. For instance, ISTPs may have a goal in mind for what they want to accomplish that day, only to discover the task much larger than they originally imagined. But because a bigger task poses a greater challenge, they take the bait and see if they can still manage to get it done. The problem, of course, is that this essentially locks them into Judging mode, since any deviation into Se Perceiving will preclude them from accomplishing their goal. This includes closing themselves off to other people, who come to be viewed as intrusions or impediments to their productivity. Consequently, ISTPs who are frequently in the grip may end up ostracizing themselves from other people.

What is interesting is that ISTPs, like other types, can be relatively unaware of falling into a grip experience, rationalizing their obsessiveness as being "efficient" or "productive." Moreover, since grip experiences are fueled by adrenaline, they can feel "good" at some level, allowing for heightened focus and endurance. At the same time, there is a part of ISTPs that knows they are in trouble. When all they can do is compulsively hurl themselves into their work, a part of them realizes this is unsustainable, unbalanced, and potentially destructive.

To compensate for the isolation involved with grip behavior, ISTPs may "crutch" their inferior Fe through their relationships, which provides the reassurance that external Fe support is available should they need it. This is why so many ISTPs (and INTPs) struggle when it comes to balancing their work and interpersonal relationships.

Slippery & Elusive Emotions

For ISTPs and INTPs alike, their Fe is rather naive and childlike. They may be easily moved by cheesy romantic comedies or sappy love songs, anything that incites their subconscious Fe emotions. They can also be easy targets for "love at first sight" sorts of infatuation. They may be particularly susceptible to being wooed by Feeling types (especially FJs), who can bypass their typical channels of logic and appeal directly to ISTPs' less conscious Fe.

Because of the inferior position of their Fe, ISTPs struggle to intentionally contact or understand their emotions. It's not they never experience emotions, but only that their emotions seem to have a mind of their own, coming and going as they please. So even if ISTPs are aware of what emotions are appropriate for a given situation, they often do not "feel" them at the time, engendering a sense of awkwardness or discomfort in emotional situations. They may even experience the desired emotion a few hours later, but it's almost as though their emotions get "stage fright" when "put on the spot." To compensate, ISTPs may try to use their Fe to offer the socially-appropriate words. But without experiencing the emotions directly, they often sound clumsy or contrived in their expressions. At times, this can be difficult for their romantic partners, particularly for FJ types, who desire a reciprocation of authentic emotional expression. But because of their Fe stage fright, ISTPs may not experience their feelings "at the right times" or can have trouble expressing them when they are present.

While ISTPs can certainly have trouble contacting their emotions, they usually have little difficulty overriding or detaching from them. Consequently, ISTPs are less apt to struggle with guilt, regret, or shame in the way that other types might. Others may even be surprised how quickly ISTPs can resume "business as usual" after what most would consider tragic or traumatic circumstances. This should not necessarily be viewed as a flaw in the ISTP, however, but merely a reflection of the unconscious nature of their Fe.

Conflict Avoidance, Passive-Aggressiveness, & Desire for Affirmation

ISTPs want everyone to feel included and to be treated with fairness and respect (Fe). While not as warm or effusive as FJ types, they are concerned with others' feelings and try to avoid hurting or offending them. They seek to maintain a basic level of harmony in their immediate circumstances.

Fe also contributes to ISTPs' desire for public affirmation. Fe involves making connections between one's own emotions and those of others. While ISTPs may not always "feel" what others are feeling their Fe still desires the sense of social affirmation and validation. Consequently, there are times when ISTPs are helpful or compliant largely for the sake of external approval or to maintain a certain public perception. ISTPs with a strong concern for their image can take social engagements quite seriously. They want others to see them as laudable employees, spouses, parents, or citizens. Their desire for public esteem can also be a motivating force in ISTPs' desire for achievement.

ISTPs' propensity for conflict-avoidance and need for affirmation, on the one hand, with their need for independence (Ti), on the other, contributes to no small number of relational difficulties. Especially when in the grip of workaholism, ISTPs may feel they don't need or want other people around. Eventually, they come to a point of feeling miserably imbalanced, which prompts them to reinitiate contact with others, at least until they fall into the grip again. This cycle of alternating between needing and devaluing others is common among ISTPs and narcissists alike.

In the name of conflict-avoidance and preservation of external harmony, ISTPs may do all they can to circumvent directly expressing their frustrations or grievances. Wittingly or not, they view conflict as a potential threat to the relationship they depend on to meet their Fe needs, as well as a threat to the flawless image they seek to preserve. So rather than giving voice (Fe) to their concerns, ISTPs prefer to analyze (Ti) or act on them (Se), sometimes in passive-aggressive ways. They may, for instance, intentionally start spending more time at the office as a passive form of rebellion against their partner. Or, they may make sudden executive decisions without giving others any say or prior notice.

Poor communication can also lead ISTPs to create a convoluted set of assumptions about what their partners think, want, and expect. Unhealthy ISTPs may spin an ever-expanding web of faulty beliefs and assumptions about their partner. In so doing, they may come to resent or otherwise think negatively of their mates, even if largely a product of their own assumptions.

Personal growth for ISTPs involves integrating their Fe through consistent and satisfying use of their Ti and Se. Integrating ISTPs must also must learn to recognize the difference between healthy modes of work versus functioning in the grip of their inferior function. Healthy work for ISTPs includes remaining open to Se experiences and diversions, which can keep them from becoming too one-track minded.

In addition to taking a healthier approach to their work, integrating ISTPs must enhance their self-awareness and communication in their relationships. This includes working to unearth all their implicit assumptions about relationships in general and their partner in particular. It means being willing to dialogue about uncomfortable topics that may produce temporary pain or conflict. It is not until they "clear the air," learning to be more open and honest with themselves and their partners, that ISTPs will experience true satisfaction and wholeness in their relationships.

INFP

The INFP personality type makes up about 5% of the general population, outnumbering INFJs at a pace of four to one. INFPs are well described as seekers. They want to understand who they are and their purpose in the world. Curious and restless, they enjoy entertaining new ideas and possibilities. They are rarely content with "what is," preferring instead to focus their sights on "what could be." This, combined with their strong idealism, can engender a sort of "grass is greener" mentality.

INFPs are among the most open-minded (and open-hearted) of the personality types. While not to the same extent as ENFPs, they often bring an experimental attitude to life as they explore a variety of ideas, lifestyles, and experiences. In each new experience, INFPs see an opportunity to not only learn about the world, but about themselves and their life's purpose.

Their curiosity about the world, including its potential role in clarifying their identity, can inspire INFPs to travel or adopt a peripatetic lifestyle. They may, for instance, choose to explore other cultures, live out of a vehicle, or take to the woods. As long as these sorts of explorations feel stimulating and life-giving, INFPs will continue to explore them, even amid pressures to embrace a more conventional path.

Jon Krakauer's captivating book, later turned movie, *Into the Wild*, details the life one such INFP seeker, Chris McCandless. McCandless was academically gifted and a recent high school graduate. While nearly everyone assumed he would head off to college and begin his path toward worldly success, McCandless had others aspirations. Something seemed to be missing from his life and from the conventional lives of those around him, that he felt he needed to pursue and understand. So instead of heading off to college, he sold most of his possessions and embarked on a life of exploration, culminating in a journey deep into the Alaskan wilderness.

Perhaps even more familiar is the account of another INFP, Henry David Thoreau, which we find in his classic work, *Walden*. Like McCandless, Thoreau was unimpressed by conventional life and dreamed of something more: "I went to the woods because I wished to live deliberately, to confront only the essential facts of life . . . and not, when it came to die, discover that I had not lived."

Like Thoreau and McCandless, INFPs seek a life of passion and intensity. They want to know what it means to be fully alive and how they might cultivate a rich and abundant life.

INFPs' seeking impetus is informed and perpetuated by their critical observations of society and culture. They often see themselves as characteristically different from, or at odds with, their surrounding culture, sometimes feeling like outsiders or misfits. They can be wary of "conventional wisdom" and societal prescriptions, preferring instead to forge their own unique path.

Amassing wealth or material goods is rarely high on INFPs' priority list. Money is valued only to the extent that it furnishes the time and freedom to explore their deepest passions. Considering the relative unimportance of material niceties to INFPs, the idea of performing uninspiring work for the sake of a paycheck is invariably off-putting to them. Consequently, they, not unlike INTPs, often adopt a minimalist lifestyle, hoping this will translate into less time spent performing uninteresting work.

As INFPs proceed in their search for self, they eventually stumble onto something that deeply moves or inspires them. They even feel they've finally found what they have been looking for. But more often than not, their enthusiasm is short-lived, once the novelty of their new discovery has worn off. Over time, this can become frustrating or demoralizing for INFPs, since they so desperately want to find themselves. They don't want to remain seekers forever. They want know to know their mission in life. They want their seeking efforts to culminate in a sense of conviction and direction for their lives.

With that said, it would be wrong to pretend that INFPs don't also find the seeker's journey deeply meaningful and enjoyable. Whether they admit it or not, their seeking is at least as much about the journey as it is the destination. But it is also true that they wouldn't be seeking, at least not with such vigor and zeal, without an anticipated payoff. Hence, they may resist notions like "just relax and enjoy the journey" because the imagined destination, that ever-elusive Holy Grail, imbues their actions with greater meaning, urgency, and intensity.

INFPs can be drawn to all sorts of creative endeavors—film, photography, poetry, music, theater, fiction writing, the fine arts, and so on. Other INFPs may opt for careers that inspire their inferior function, Extraverted Thinking (Te), such as science, computers, engineering, law, economics, etc. Regardless of how they start their career journey, many will continue to function as seekers for years, even decades. They often find themselves most inspired when working on their own personal projects, which allow them to pursue their own interests with full freedom and authenticity. Many will dabble in freelancing while dreaming of the time when they can cut ties with their day job and pursue their passion on a full-time basis.

INFPs' Functional Stack & Personality Type Development

INFPs' functional stack includes the following functions:

Dominant: Introverted Feeling (Fi)

Auxiliary: Extraverted Intuition (Ne)

Tertiary: Introverted Sensing (Si)

Inferior: Extraverted Thinking (Te)

INFPs' personality type development consists of three primary phases:

Phase I (Childhood)

Phase I is characterized by the exploration and development of INFPs' dominant function, Introverted Feeling (Fi). Even as children, INFPs are often "highly sensitive persons" (HSPs). Sensitive to their own feelings, as well as those of others, they feel unsettled and anxious in conflictual situations. This may prompt them to seek refuge in time alone, finding comfort in solitary activities such as daydreaming, reading, drawing, listening to music, etc. Hence, young INFPs come to enjoy exploring their own interests, free from external disruptions. In time, they develop a unique sense of self through exploring their feelings (Fi) and imagination (Ne).

Phase II (Adolescence-30s)

Phase II involves additional development of their auxiliary function (Ne), as well as heightened polarity and conflict between their dominant Fi and their inferior function, Extraverted Thinking (Te).

While INFPs do function as seekers as children, in the sense of exploring the world through their feelings and imagination, their seeking tendencies (Ne) grow more intense and explicit as they approach adulthood. This is prompted, at least to some extent, by concerns about adulthood, which cause them to think more seriously about the trajectory of their life.

Ne is INFPs' preferred extraverted function and one of the primary tools they use to explore the outside world. These explorations may include things like dabbling in countercultures, experimenting with drugs, starting their own band, travelling overseas, joining the Peace Corps, etc. Through these experiences, they hope to get a better sense of who they are and where they might fit into the world. Through this process of world exploration (which is equally, if not more, about self-exploration) many INFPs will either modify or part ways with the religious and political views they were raised with.

The liberal and explorative ways of Ne are checked and countered by INFPs' tertiary Si and inferior Te, which urge them to "be responsible" and follow a more traditional path. INFPs who heed this prompting will function more conventionally (e.g., finish their degree, get a job, get married, etc.) and may look less like seekers. They may, however, be more disposed to a mid-life identity crisis if they conclude that the path they chose was not authentically their own.

Perhaps most commonly, Phase II INFPs feel themselves bouncing between unconventional (Fi-Ne) and conventional (Si-Te) paths as they try to discern what works best for them. While other types must also find a way of reconciling opposing forces within themselves, INFPs (along with INTPs) tend to be most aware that they are on a journey of self-discovery and self-development.

Phase III (30s, 40s, & Beyond)

Phase III represents the well-integrated personality. According to Elaine Schallock, integration occurs when the functional stack is consistently used in a "top-down" fashion. By this she means that the functions are best prioritized and utilized in a dominant-auxiliary-tertiary-inferior sequence. If used consistently over time, she suggests the top-down approach will naturally result in greater development and integration of all the functions. In Schallock's view, "jumping the stack," that is, trying to appease or satisfy the inferior function directly or through various short-cuts, is rarely a reliable or sustainable means to integration.

The first and probably most important step for INFPs seeking integration is learning how to effectively transition into Ne perceiving. To understand why this is so critical, we must remember that Fi is not only an introverted function, but also a judging function (all the T and F functions are judging functions). Therefore, counterbalancing Fi requires both extraversion and perceiving. And this is precisely what Ne, which is an extraverted perceiving function, can do for INFPs.

There are two reasons why Ne may be a more reasonable solution to integration for INFPs than Te. The first is that Te is not a perceiving function and therefore cannot provide the same degree of counterbalance to Fi as Ne does. The second reason is Te is deeply buried in INFPs' subconscious, which prevents them from readily accessing and integrating it. This is why Schallock's top-down approach (i.e., Fi to Ne to Si to Te) is a more effective route to integration than jumping the stack (i.e., jumping from Fi to Te).

INFPs who have learned how to truly perceive and/or create through Ne discover a welcome alternative to the bipolar leaps between Fi and Te they experience in Phase II. Effectively transitioning into Ne often induces a state of "flow," which is the inner experience of integration. In the flow state, INFPs forget about themselves and their concerns, becoming "one" with the activity at hand. They are neither over nor under-stimulated, and their worries tend to fade into the background.

Phase III INFPs have a clearer sense of who they are and how they can live most authentically and effectively. This allows them to feel more safe, secure, and grounded in themselves as well as, if by some act of magic, in the world.

INFPs' Dominant Function: Introverted Feeling (Fi)

INFPs are deeply aware of and in touch with their inner landscape. Their dominant Fi is inwardly focused and adept at evaluating and handling their personal tastes, values, and emotions. Because Fi is introverted in direction, INFPs process their emotions and experiences on a largely independent basis. With each new feeling, experience, or idea they evaluate, their sense of self becomes a little clearer. This was nicely enumerated by one of our blog readers:

> *"My inner values and feelings (Fi) are like a building, a structure of affections that inform my worldview. This involves an inner love for certain things, and an inner repulsion for other things. My values and feelings form "blocks" of varying hardness, depending on how strongly I feel about them; the stronger ones are more resilient . . . I constantly discover more about the structure as I go, and what I should change to make it better. For example, I didn't have to factually discern a respect for human dignity; I simply found myself in situations where people did not respect human dignity, and it made me angry — I found out that I hate bullying."*

By reflecting on the experiences of life, whether gleaned from fiction or real life, INFPs come to better understand themselves. Despite this journey toward deeper understanding, INFPs often feel that their self-understanding remains incomplete. They may still feel they don't know themselves well enough to wholeheartedly commit to a certain path in life. And they feel it is only through a more complete or definite self-understanding that they will be capable of acting with full authenticity and conviction.

In addition to its role in shaping INFPs' self-understanding and identity, Fi can develop deep attachments and loyalties to certain externalities. INFPs are particularly prone to empathize with and develop attachments to those unable to help or care for themselves—animals, children, the less fortunate, victims of injustice, etc. They can often be found caring for the elderly, sick, disabled, and disenfranchised. Animal lovers to the core, they shower their pets with affection while also showing deep concern for strays. If sufficiently moved or inspired, INFPs may also take up a niche cause, such as garnering research funding for a rare disease affecting a loved one. Finally, many INFPs want (or will eventually want) their own children. Children can serve as a reliable and rewarding lifelong investment for INFPs' love and attention.

Due to the introverted nature of Fi, INFPs' status as feelers is not always evident from without. When immersed in Fi, they can seem a bit cool, aloof, or indifferent. In *Psychological Types*, Jung described the introverted Feeler (i.e., IFPs) in the following way:

> *"They are mostly silent, inaccessible, hard to understand; often they hide behind a childish or banal mask, and their temperament is inclined to melancholy . . . Their outward demeanor is harmonious, inconspicuous . . . with no desire to affect others, to impress, influence or change them in any way. If this is more pronounced, it arouses suspicion of indifference and coldness . . . Although there is a constant readiness for peaceful and harmonious co-existence, strangers are shown no touch of amiability, no gleam of responsive warmth . . . It might seem on a superficial view that they have no feelings at all."*

Of course, this sort of outer presentation belies what we know about INFPs' inner world, which is abundant with life and feeling. It is also true that many INFPs compensate for their lack of Extraverted

Feeling (Fe) by invoking their auxiliary Ne. When wielding Ne, INFPs are more outwardly open, receptive, quirky, and engaging.

INFPs' Auxiliary Function: Extraverted Intuition (Ne)

Ne demands novelty. It craves new ideas, connections, and possibilities. It seeks to understand the world (and the self) through the lens of ideas. It therefore comes as no surprise that Ne plays a prominent role in INFPs' search for self.

Among Ne's manifold talents is its knack for sniffing out intriguing possibilities. As we've seen, INFPs commonly assume the role of wanderer or seeker. Rarely do they know exactly what they are seeking, which is largely why operating in Ne mode can be exhilarating. Ne can be associated with a sense of blind anticipation and expectation, of not knowing who or what will manifest next in one's life journey. INFPs relish the sense of adventure, expectancy, and wonderment conferred by Ne. This is one reason they enjoy traveling. The idea of exploring nature or different cultures feels rife with possibilities. A serendipitous encounter with a kindred spirit, the discovery of a life-changing book, finding inspiration through ancient art and architecture, such are the anticipated rewards of following Ne.

Ne can function either expressively or receptively. The verbal expression of Ne amounts to something like "brainstorming aloud." When speaking, INFPs may at times struggle to make their point, as Ne bounces from one idea or association to the next. Even ideas that seem inwardly cogent to the INFP may scatter when expressed, like a ray of light passing through a prism.

On a more positive note, INFPs often capitalize on the divergent and diversifying effects of Ne through inspired works of art or innovation. Whether they realize or not, INFPs are among the most profoundly creative of all types.

When operating receptively, Ne prompts INFPs to gather information. It scans for new patterns, associations, and possibilities. INFPs commonly exercise this side of their Ne through activities such as reading, research, entertainment, and conversation with others.

In engaging with others, INFPs enjoy asking probing questions. They find it interesting to explore the unique qualities of every individual, as well as the life story that explains or gives context to those characteristics. Hence, INFPs are typically viewed as good listeners as well as facilitators of conversation. Others sense and appreciate that the INFP is authentically interested in understanding them for who they are as individuals, and that they are doing so in a non-threatening and non-judgmental way.

Like INTPs, INFPs have a love-hate relationship with their Ne. They relish the sense of wonder, curiosity, and anticipation it instills, as well as its creativity and openness. Without their Ne, they would not be the seekers and creatives that they are. But living with Ne is not without its challenges. For one, it can make it difficult for INFPs to arrive at firm conclusions or make important life decisions. It often seems that at the very moment they feel confident about a given conclusion or decision, Ne finds a way to inject doubt and uncertainty. This can be frustrating for INFPs who feel they are working so hard to find their rightful place in the world. At times, Ne may even cause them to worry that they have made no real progress toward anything substantial, or worse, that they may never find what they are looking for.

INFPs' Tertiary Function: Introverted Sensing (Si)

Introverted Sensing (Si) is a conservative function. It engenders a concern and respect for the past—for what is routine, familiar, or traditional.

While INFPs may appreciate some amount of routine in their lives, such as devoting a certain time of day to creative work, they are less inclined to wholeheartedly embrace traditions or conventions in the manner of SJ types. For INFPs, a full embrace of tradition can only emerge authentically after they explore it (and its alternatives) through the lens of Fi and Ne. So even when a given tradition manages to pass muster, it is only after INFPs have personalized it and made it their own, interpreting it in a way that resonates with their deepest values.

The influence of Si may also be reflected in INFPs' attitudes toward money and material goods. INFPs are often minimalists with respect to possessions. Many opt for rather simple living arrangements so they can devote more time and energy to pursuing their true passions. This tendency toward material minimalism is often discernible in their style of dress and artistic preferences. Namely, their approach often entails the creative reuse or recombination (Ne) of pre-existing resources (Si) to fashion something new. In this spirit, many INFPs supply their wardrobes, homes, and art rooms with items from thrift shops, antique stores, or garage sales.

An oft overlooked feature of Si is its role in the perception of internal bodily sensations—the body as felt and experienced from within. Si can be associated with the raw and basic sense of "being" that exists apart from thought or outward stimuli. Historically, Eastern philosophical and religious traditions have led the way in exploring this domain of human experience through practices such as yoga, Tai-Chi, or meditation. Because of INFPs' openness to new experiences (Ne), as well as their desire to explore the mind-body connection and enhance their sense of well-being, many are drawn to these sorts of holistic practices (especially yoga).

Finally, what may be the most important benefit of Si for INFPs is its role in consolidating and recalling past experiences and life lessons. It can therefore keep INFPs from repeating past mistakes and help them clarify their future direction. Exploring evidence from the past can instill greater confidence in who they are and what they care about, aiding the consolidation and crystallization of their self-concept.

INFPs' Inferior Function: Extraverted Thinking (Te)

Because the inferior function operates on a largely unconscious level, all types struggle to understand and develop it. This function represents a strange and unfamiliar land, one that is difficult to consistently access, which is why it is sometimes called the "lost" or "missing" function. It is often symbolized in dreams as something deep underground, undersea, or in a dark forest. Despite its relative unconsciousness, the psychospiritual importance of the inferior function should not be underestimated. Indeed, it plays a surprisingly influential role in the motivations and developmental trajectory of each personality type. Its sense of novelty and mystery can make it a powerful source of energy and motivation.

For INFPs, the allure of their inferior function, Extraverted Thinking (Te), is illustrated in their frequent attraction to characteristically T careers such as math, science, law, economics, computers, accounting, engineering, and the like. The most "left-brained" of all functions, Te can be associated with structure, organization, quantification, and the ability to manage T things, such as time and finances. The concerns of Te are myriad, spanning from the laws of physics, to state and federal laws, to workplace policies and procedures, to time management, to household organization.

As an extraverted Judging function, Te also serves as a tool for verbally asserting, in a measured and deliberate way, one's opinions and judgments. Unlike Extraverted Feeling (Fe), it is unemotional in its presentation, showing little variation in intonation or physical expression. At times, the measured and rational character of Te may cause INFPs to be mistaken for Thinking types.

While INFPs are often characterized as impractical and disorganized, this is not necessarily how they want to operate or see themselves. The truth is most INFPs like the idea of imposing some sort of order on their existence. They intuitively realize that external structure is to some extent necessary for them to live happy and healthy lives. INFPs who are parents, for instance, quickly discover that it is difficult to develop an optimal parent-child relationship in a chaotic household. However, because Te is not INFPs' natural strength, they often struggle to maintain their preferred level of order and organization. Many report difficulty handling logistical details, staying on top of their finances, organizing their homes and schedules, or developing effective rules and modes of discipline for their children.

My INFP cousin, for instance, once recounted her experience of flying her cat on an airline. She recalled taking great care to ensure that her cat had everything it needed to be safe and comfortable in its carrier. Unfortunately, she failed to take note of the airline's proof of animal vaccination requirement. In type parlance, she had used her Fi and Te to ensure the cat's needs were met, but fell short with respect to the extraneous Si-Te details of the situation.

INFPs may also struggle to accurately assess the quantity of resources required for a given situation. I've observed several INFPs, for instance, who have either overestimated or underestimated the amount of food required for feeding a group of people or the number of beds needed to comfortably accommodate them. Assuming that everything will somehow work itself out, INFPs may fail to take the time to accurately plan or quantify things ahead of time. This can be frustrating for guests who feel their needs are not being met, but who are uncomfortable asking the INFP to remedy his or her oversights.

I have also known INFPs to be poor assessors of time. On a number of occasions, I've seen them underestimate the amount of time required for a given task, such as registering their car at the motor vehicle office. And because of these sorts of miscalculations, they often find themselves frantically scrambling to manage their other scheduled obligations.

In short, just as NT types can appear naïve or incompetent with respect to SF matters (e.g., parenting or interpersonal relationships), so it is with INFPs in their ST affairs. Of course, this truth is rarely easy for INFPs to hear. As is true of all types, the inferior function can be a touchy or sensitive area for INFPs. This is especially true for those who feel they have worked hard to remediate their Te shortcomings, such as by reading books on parenting methods, organization strategies, money management, etc. INFPs can get really excited when learning a new Te strategy or method, perhaps even developing plans for its implementation. However, because of its dependence on their inferior function, INFPs often fail to consistently or effectively implement it, thereby lengthening their list of unactualized good intentions.

In most cases, INFPs manage to do a good job handling some portion of their Te affairs. They may, for instance, manage to maintain an organized workstation or discover a method for being more punctual. These "small wins" allow them to feel that at least part of their lives is under control. However, when faced with a multitude of Te demands—maintaining an orderly household, personal finances, remembering birthdays, workplace responsibilities, etc.—they can easily feel overwhelmed.

Head (Te) vs. Heart (Fi)

One of the more common misconceptions about INFPs is that they care mostly about values or morals, but little about truth. The reality is that some INFPs value truth (i.e., Te) so much that they view their life's purpose as a search for truth. Consider, for instance, the following quotes from my INFP friend's blog: "I just want the world to make sense . . . I use the intellect to justify my existence . . . I worship at the altar of truth . . . Truth is my religion . . . I want truth to matter to other people."

Similarly, in his novel, *Emile*, the 18th-century INFP writer, Jean Jacques Rousseau, penned: "I am not a great philosopher, and I care little to be one. But I sometimes have good sense, and I always love the truth."

Despite their professed love for truth, INFPs often feel that truth, especially that which is logic based (Te), can be hard to come by. This is intimated in Rousseau's *Confessions*: "I have a passionate temperament and lively, headstrong emotions. Yet my thoughts arise slowly and confusedly, and are never ready until too late. It is as if my heart and my brain did not belong to the same person."

To compensate for an unreliable T function, Rousseau, in *Emile*, urged that attention be directed to the condition of the heart (F): "I do not want to argue with you or even attempt to convince you. It is enough for me to reveal to you what I think in the simplicity of my heart. Consult yours during my speech. That is all I ask of you." Rousseau hoped that purity of intention, including the earnest desire for truth, could somehow substitute for any lack of T prowess.

Art (Fi) vs. Science (Te)

As exemplified in Rousseau's vocation as a writer, one way INFPs go about reconciling Fi and Te is through creative pursuits. Of all the arts, writing, especially non-fiction writing, is one of the more obvious means of incorporating the Te element. In other arts, such as music or fiction writing, the opportunity for T-F integration is also present, but is more subtle and circuitous.

One of the most important benefits of creative work for INFPs is its ability to incorporate their auxiliary Ne. For all types, the auxiliary function (as well as the tertiary) serves an important bridge between the dominant and inferior function. Because Ne is more conscious and accessible than Te is for INFPs, it is easier for them to develop and integrate. While reaching Te by way of Ne and Si may seem longer and less immediately gratifying than trying to access Te directly, it typically proves more satisfying and sustainable over the long haul. Instead of bouncing between the extremes of Fi and Te, Fi and Ne can more easily work as a team, allowing INFPs to routinely achieve integration through creative work.

With that said, many INFPs will nonetheless opt for more direct routes to Te by pursuing characteristically T-oriented careers such as math, science, law, economics, computers, engineering, etc. While some of these fields do incorporate Ne and may prove satisfying for some INFPs, in many cases, INFPs ultimately discover that their Fi needs are not being met. This may compel them to begin searching for an entirely different career or to explore ways of reworking their current career to allow for greater incorporation of Fi and Ne.

Subjective (Fi) vs. Objective (Te) Values

On a broader level, INFPs may experience an ongoing tension between the subjective values of their Fi and the objective values of Te. Namely, Fi urges INFPs to follow their heart, including their own subjective tastes and values. Te, by contrast, may impel INFPs to "be responsible," follow the rules, or "do things by the book."

INFPs are therefore bound to struggle in situations where their personal values are in conflict with external demands or expectations. This may prove true for INFPs still living at home with their parents, as well in school, the workplace, or other relationships. Fi, especially combined when Ne, seeks to maximize personal freedom and autonomy (this is often particularly pronounced in INFP males). This may at times inspire a rebellious attitude toward authority, potentially even compelling INFPs to quit their jobs or drop out of school.

Other INFPs seem more tolerant of Te rules and structure, even to the point of assuming predominantly administrative work roles. According to *The MBTI Manual*, however, INFPs' first vocational preference is to perform creative rather than administrative work. Hence, even INFPs who have learned to tolerate Te administrative duties may not be fully satisfied in their careers.

Fairness (Fi) in Systems (Te)

INFPs also commonly gravitate toward non-profit work. Working for a non-profit organization seems to be a rather obvious way for them to marry their Fi values with their Te's interest in improving systems. More specifically, INFPs want to ensure that individual rights and liberties (Fi) are respected and protected within the system (Te), especially for individuals with special needs or challenges. So when INFPs encounter a system-related injustice they feel strongly about, they will often take up the cause and work toward Te reform. We see this all the time, for instance, when Fi tragedies (e.g., school shootings, child abductions) prompt the passing of new laws (Te) or new non-profit initiatives intended to prevent future recurrences.

Managing Oneself (Fi) vs. Managing Others (Te)

As we've seen, Fi is adept at navigating and managing INFPs' emotional landscape. Hence, INFPs often have a strong internal locus of control, feeling they are more than capable of taking care of themselves. This is one reason why they may struggle to work under the leadership of others. They crave autonomy and want to be free to follow the lead of Fi.

In an organizational setting, therefore, taking a position in management may seem, at least at first blush, to be a reasonable solution to their desire for more autonomy. INFPs may also enjoy the status associated with management, perhaps feeling it sets them apart or signifies their intelligence (their inferior Te can crave recognition for intelligence). Unfortunately, becoming a manager rarely solves the Fi-Te problem.

For one, INFPs still find that they must answer to someone else and therefore can't enjoy full autonomy. Second, management places heavy demands on their Te that they may not be naturally well equipped to handle. Namely, it requires the ability to be outwardly assertive and directive, and to routinely and directly deal with conflict. And due to the fact that INFPs' Te is inferior, these duties can prove difficult and taxing for INFPs.

INFPs commonly struggle to "put their foot down" and say what they really think. More often, they opt to swallow their judgments and work through the issue on an independent basis. Instead of expressing their concerns directly, they often do so more obliquely and passively, such as through a combination of hints, leading questions, and actions. They then hope that others will be able to "read between the lines" in order to understand their concern. Their discomfort with extraverting judgment also contributes to their tendency to avoid interpersonal conflict whenever possible.

Of all types, INFPs are among the most likely to agree with Aldous Huxley's confession that "there is only one corner of the universe you can be certain of improving, and that's your own self." It is therefore ironic that so many INFPs seem to end up in management roles. The fact that an INFP would even consider management may thus seem perplexing to those who know them well. But this choice becomes more understandable when we understand the Fi-Te struggle that underlies it.

Parent (Fi) vs. Careerist (Te)

Fi-Te dynamics also come to the fore in navigating a satisfying work-life balance. On the one hand, INFP parents typically want to spend as much time with their children as possible. This often includes staying at home during their early years to ensure the formation of secure child-parent bonds. On the other hand, INFPs may feel compelled to work because of circumstantial demands (e.g., finances) or because of their own psychological needs.

Of course, there are no easy answers to this issue. Some INFPs may opt to put off having children until they find themselves and their vocational path, while others may take the parenting plunge at an early age, perhaps figuring they can do more self-reflection later in life or while they are raising their children.

ISFP

ISFPs comprise about 8-9% of the general population, making them one of the more commonly encountered personality types.

ISFPs are lovers, nurturers, and caregivers. They experience great joy from spending time and making memories with their friends and loved ones. Like INFPs, they have a particular fondness for children and animals, as their dominant function, Introverted Feeling (Fi), is drawn to those incapable of helping themselves.

ISFPs form deep emotional attachments to their loved ones, contributing to a strong sense of loyalty and devotion. ISFPs are generally less focused on the well-being of the masses (a concern of Fe and/or Intuitive types) than they are with applying their Fi in more local and concrete ways.

Both INFPs and ISFPs are sensitive to injustices and dehumanization (Fi). While perceived injustices may motivate INFPs to write poetry or novels (Fi-Ne), ISFPs are more apt to respond with action and hands-on aid (Se). An ISFP friend of mine, for instance, works in inner-city Berkeley providing food and other goods to the homeless.

Like ESFPs, ISFPs often display a high concern for, as well as good taste in, fashion and aesthetics. They are often physically attractive, well-manicured, and enjoy keeping up their appearance. INFPs, by contrast, are often well-described as "earthy" and are far less concerned with enhancing, embellishing, or carefully attending to their physical presentation. Therefore, ISFPs and INFPs can often be distinguished rather quickly by mere observation of their physical presentation.

ISFPs commonly display impressive kinesthetic intelligence. They are often athletic and endowed with good dexterity and hand-eye coordination. In contrast to INFPs, who exhibit high levels of mental energy, ISFPs possess more physical energy and stamina. While INFPs use their Ne to explore and manufacture new ideas, ISFPs employ their hands, body, and other senses to explore and manipulate the physical world (Se).

Like other IP types, ISFPs are quite independent and self-motivated. Their sense of values (Fi), as well as their desire to excel performance-wise (Se), can motivate them to diligently and seriously apply themselves. However, because of their preference for hands-on activities, some may underperform in academic settings. As is true of other Sensing types, being forced to deal in abstractions for too long can be draining for ISFPs.

ISFPs often seem more optimistic and easily satisfied with life than INFPs. INFPs frequently have a depressive or melancholic bent, struggling to make it in a world that seems indifferent to the "impractical" (N) gifts they have to offer. ISFPs, by contrast, seem to more easily assimilate themselves to conventional careers and lifestyles.

ISFPs' Functional Stack & Type Development

ISFPs' functional stack is composed of the following functions:

Dominant: Introverted Feeling (Fi)

Auxiliary: Extraverted Sensing (Se)

Tertiary: Introverted Intuition (Ni)

Inferior: Extraverted Thinking (Te)

ISFPs' personality type development can be broadly conceived as consisting of three phases:

Phase I (Childhood)

This phase of development is characterized by the emergence of Introverted Feeling (Fi) as ISFPs' dominant personality function. Phase I ISFPs are quick to make Fi judgments, even if keeping most of their opinions and sentiments to themselves. ISFPs are also prone to viewing things in terms of black and white in this phase of their type development.

Phase II (Adolescence-30s)

Once ISFPs' dominant Fi reaches a certain threshold of strength and dominance, their inferior function, Extraverted Thinking (Te), begins to assert itself and play a more significant and mischievous role. This will be elaborated later in this profile.

Phase II ISFPs also show increasing use and development of their auxiliary function, Extraverted Sensing (Se). Their Se compels them to seek out new sensations, interests, and experiences. As a Perceiving function, it also facilitates an opening of their Fi judgments to see if they pass the test of lived experience. Phase II ISFPs may also begin to tap into their tertiary function, Introverted Intuition (Ni). Ni can subconsciously assist ISFPs in piecing together their Se experiences into a clearer and more coherent worldview.

Phase III (30s, 40s, & Beyond)

If all goes well and they are fortunate enough to enter Phase III, ISFPs become increasingly aware of the insidious ways of their inferior Te. As they become more aware of their inferior and learn to function more authentically as ISFPs, they experience greater balance between their Fi and Te. They learn that integrating their Te happens naturally and indirectly as they go about authentically using their Fi and Se. As they cultivate conditions that support their natural strengths, Phase III ISFPs come to experience a heightened sense of peace, wholeness, and satisfaction.

ISFPs' Dominant Function: Introverted Feeling (Fi)

ISFPs' dominant function is Introverted Feeling (Fi). Compared with Extraverted Feeling (Fe), Fi is more intensive, individualized, and idiosyncratic. Since Fi judgments are formed independent of collective sentiments, ISFPs may be wary of Fe judgments and expressions, which, from an Fi perspective, may seem generic, fake, or contrived.

Rightly or not, Fi is commonly perceived as more emotionally "mature" than Fe. For ISFPs, as well as other FP types, emotions are not readily expressed or dramatized. Instead, they are typically managed internally or repackaged and expressed via Extraverted Thinking (Te). Consequently, ISFPs are outwardly measured and rational in their presentation; outsiders may even mistake them for Thinking types.

The same introverted property which provides emotional restraint is also responsible for the depth and intensity of Fi. At times, one might glimpse such intensity of emotion passing through ISFPs' Te in the form of biting or caustic remarks.

Since Fi is a Judging function, it is characteristically more serious than it is light and playful. It is therefore unsurprising that ISFPs often take themselves and their lives quite seriously. In this respect, they differ from ESFPs, whose dominant function (Se) is more fun-loving and excitement-seeking. While both types utilize Se and Fi, ESFPs' are primarily geared to absorb, experience, and respond to the world (Se), whereas ISFPs are more intentional in their approach. Finding it difficult to relax and do nothing, ISFPs excel at constantly busying themselves with tasks and other matters.

ISFPs' Auxiliary Function: Extraverted Sensing (Se)

Extraverted Sensing (Se) serves as ISFPs' auxiliary function. It attunes to concrete sensory details of the external world by way of the five senses (i.e., sight, smell, touch, sound, and taste). Se types can often be found scanning the environment for interesting sensory novelties, noticing details other types might miss. They often display a strong visual recall, or what is sometimes dubbed a "photographic" memory.

Se differs from Ne in that it is not a highly verbal function. While INFPs enjoy discussing ideas, ISFPs often prefer to be "doing" something. While INFPs love playing with words or abstractions, ISFPs may get swept up in sports, performance, cooking, etc. Despite these abstract versus concrete differences, both ISFPs and INFPs are commonly considered "artistic." Unlike IJs, who outwardly express Judging (Fe or Te), IPs extravert their Perceiving function (Se or Ne). This can lead IPs to appear more creative or artistic. With regard to creative expression, INFPs are inclined toward writing or poetry, while ISFPs are often better suited for painting, sculpting, or various types of performance.

Especially in F types, Se contributes to a strong concern for taste, aesthetics, and fashion. As mentioned earlier, ISFPs are more concerned with their appearance and more liberal users of make-up or other embellishments than INFPs (who use Si) tend to be. Not only is Se associated with taste, but because it is extraverted, it gravitates toward *popular* tastes and fashions. This creates an interesting dynamic in ISFPs. On the one hand, their Fi is highly individualized, concerned with making its own value judgments and developing its own tastes. On the other hand, their Se encourages them to notice what everyone else is doing and to follow suit. Because Fi is dominant, however, we would expect it to win out most of the time.

The Fi-Se combination may also inspire ISFPs to develop refined tastes for food or drink. Many enjoy cooking, wine tasting, and sampling new cuisines and restaurants. Contrast this with INFPs, whose Ne-Si combination inspires a more basic diet, often centered on organic or whole foods.

Se can also be associated with broad interests in sports or other "hands-on" activities. It may compel ISFPs to take up work as chefs, artisans, dancers, musicians, physical and occupational therapists, and the like.

ISFPs' Tertiary Function: Introverted Intuition (Ni)

Like ISTPs, ISFPs use Introverted Intuition (Ni) as their tertiary function, which may lead them to develop some degree of interest in abstract or theoretical topics. After all, Ni and Fi are the two introverted functions employed by INTJs, who are among the most theoretically-minded of all types. However, because ISFPs' Ni is tertiary rather than dominant, it is far less accessible for conscious intuitive perception. So like other SP types, ISFPs gain most of their insights through lived experience rather than through bursts of intuitive knowing.

ISFPs' Inferior Function: Extraverted Thinking (Te)

As is true of other types, ISFPs can be easily blinded to the degree to which their inferior function impacts their decisions and behavior. Without sufficient awareness and integration of their inferior, ISFPs will continue to feel incomplete and be prone to unwise decision-making in their careers and relationships. Therefore, ISFPs must work to understand the ways in which their inferior function, Extraverted Thinking (Te), manifests in their personality.

For both ISFPs and INFPs, the Fi-Te function pair involves a tension between individuality and subjectivity (Fi), on the one hand, and standardized ways of doing things (Te), on the other. Consciously, ISFPs tend to emphasize the former, championing the unique values and preferences of the individual (Fi). Unconsciously, however, they are drawn to "objective" truths and more standardized ways of doing things (Te).

Since all Introverts' inferior function is extraverted in direction, it is sensitive to externalities. For ISFPs, their inferior Te is attuned to the structure of external systems, systems that are inextricably linked with Fi-related concerns such as hunger, homelessness, or other injustices. This is one of the chief ways their Te works with their Fi. Their Te draws conclusions about external circumstances and their Fi provides the subjective response to those Te judgments. The world relies on ISFPs (and INFPs) to use this Te-Fi process to identify potential injustices and to ensure that the individual (Fi) doesn't get lost in the system (Te).

ISFPs' Te can also contribute a desire to organize the immediate environment. Like INFPs, ISFPs can derive a great deal of guilty pleasure from ordering and organizing, giving their Te the sense of external control it desires.

Te may also inspire ISFPs to "follow the rules" and "be responsible." ISFPs who regularly indulge their Te may be so bent on being pious or responsible that they fail to spend sufficient time exploring and experiencing life (Se). And because responsibility is culturally endorsed as a positive virtue, they may fail to realize that being obsessed with it is actually quite unhealthy for them, forfeiting their openness to new experiences and potentially some degree of compassion (Fi). In the grip of Te, ISFPs can become rigid, particular, and dogmatic, appearing more like ESTJs than ISFPs.

ISFPs feel they have little control over the outside world. Like other IPs, ISFPs are known for their lack of assertiveness and conflict avoidance. This is partly due to their Fi's desire to avoid hurting others' feelings. It also relates to the fact that being "assertive" involves extraverted Judging, which for ISFPs, is in the inferior position (Te). So when it comes to expressing their judgments, they often avoid doing so directly. Instead, they may simply swallow the judgment and try to deal with its attendant feelings by way of their Fi. Or, they may address the issue more obliquely through action (Se). Like other P-types, ISFPs can be disposed to expressing their grievances through passive-aggressive behavior.

For ISFPs, personal growth requires regular employment of their dominant Fi and auxiliary Se. It involves avoiding obsessing over Te responsibilities and, instead, building a life based on care and empathy (Fi), as well as a breadth of activities (Se). Those who do so successfully are more open, flexible, and balanced, capable of avoiding the traps and pitfalls of the inferior function.

ISFJ

ISFJs are among the more commonly encountered personality types, thought to comprise upwards of 8% of the general population. To understand ISFJs, we must first consider their dominant function, Introverted Sensing (Si), which compels them to preserve and protect past ways of doing things. This is why David Keirsey has dubbed them "guardians." Like other SJ types, they grow attached to the routine, familiar, and expected. The more often they do something in a particular way (e.g., eat a certain type of meal for lunch), the harder it is for them to break out of that pattern. The same can be said of their beliefs and worldview. As adults, ISFJs often persist in the beliefs and worldview of their childhood. In sum, they can be seen to rely heavily on past precedent, both behaviorally and ideationally.

While sometimes viewed as stubborn or nitpicky, ISFJs are actually more easygoing than they are often given credit for. Since their dominant function (Si) is a Perceiving function, they are naturally inclined to assume a receptive rather than a controlling role. Unfortunately, this often goes unnoticed by the casual onlooker, since Si is introverted in direction. Especially in their free time, ISFJs know how to be leisurely, something ESFJs can have a harder time with.

In sharing the identical set of psychological functions, ISFJs resemble ESFJs. One difference is ESFJs tend to be more warm and engaging upfront, while ISFJs can be a bit more reserved and take longer to warm-up. These two types also differ with respect to inferior function issues, with ISFJs wrestling with Ne and ESFJs with Ti.

ISFJs also resemble ISTJs, since they share the same dominant and inferior function. However, their auxiliary functions do confer significant differences. ISFJs use Extraverted Feeling (Fe) as their auxiliary function, which grants them a greater measure of social intelligence. While ISTJs may lack some degree of social grace, their auxiliary Te contributes stronger powers of logical and tactical intelligence. ISFJs' Fe may also contribute an added measure of open-mindedness, at least outwardly. However, this may be more a matter of ISFJs' concern for interpersonal harmony than a true difference in openness.

Although differing by only one "preference" (i.e., J-P), ISFJs actually share *zero* functions with ISFPs. ISFPs, who use Se instead of Si, are less concerned with past precedent than ISFJs are. And because of their Fi, ISFPs are more individualistic and less objective in their judging process. Their Se also confers a greater interest in sensory and material novelty. Moreover, ISFPs are inclined toward "hands-on" or what is described as "Realistic" work on the Holland career inventory. ISFJs, by contrast, are typically less interested in getting their hands dirty. They are more apt to pursue "Conventional" than Realistic careers. While both ISFJs and ISFPs may take up "Social" sorts of work, ISFJs gravitate toward more abstract occupations, such as teaching, whereas ISFPs, prefer more hands-on careers, such as nursing. ISFJs also make effective managers of people, balancing care and concern with organizational know-how.

All in all, ISFJs are among the most loyal, dutiful, and responsible of all types. They are admired for their devotion and steadfastness. They make loyal friends and companions, especially for those with similar values and lifestyles.

ISFJs' Functional Stack & Type Development

ISFJs' functional stack is composed of the following functions:

Dominant: Introverted Sensing (Si)

Auxiliary: Extraverted Feeling (Fe)

Tertiary: Introverted Thinking (Ti)

Inferior: Extraverted Intuition (Ne)

ISFJs' personality type development can be broadly conceived as consisting of three phases:

Phase I (Childhood)

Phase I is characterized by the development and rise to power of ISFJs' dominant function, Introverted Sensing (Si). ISFJs use their Si to absorb, integrate, and reflect on acquired information and personal experiences. Phase I ISFJs may also show some development of their auxiliary function, Extraverted Feeling (Fe), which can serve as a helpful extraverted tool for navigating and managing the outside world.

Phase II (Adolescence-30s)

While the inferior function is not entirely dormant or inert in Phase I, the epic tug-of-war between the dominant and inferior does not come to the fore until Phase II. Once ISFJs' dominant Si reaches a certain threshold of strength and dominance, their inferior function, Extraverted Intuition (Ne), begins to assert itself and play a more prominent and mischievous role. This will be elaborated later in this profile.

Phase II ISFJs also show increasing use and development of their Fe, allowing them to form and express judgments. They may even begin to tap into their tertiary function, Introverted Thinking (Ti), which serves to cross-check and refine their Fe judgments.

Phase III (30s, 40s, & Beyond)

If all goes well and they are fortunate enough to enter Phase III, ISFJs become increasingly aware of the insidious ways of their inferior Ne. As they become more aware of their inferior and learn to function more healthily as ISFJs, they experience greater balance between their Si and Ne, as well as an increasing sense of peace and wholeness.

ISFJs' Dominant Function: Introverted Sensing (Si)

ISFJs use Introverted Sensing (Si) as their dominant function. Si is the function that undergirds ISFJs' propensity to function as guardians and conservators of tradition. The longer they are immersed in particular set of circumstances, the more difficult it can be for them to open themselves to alternatives. Because Si is a Perceiving function, ISFJs are less inclined to function as frontline activists for their beliefs than ESJs, whose dominant function is a Judging function. Instead, ISFJs prefer to spend time reflecting on the past or their cherished traditions. Many enjoy attending religious services or studying religious texts, activities that strengthen and bolster their Si beliefs.

One of the most commonly overlooked features of Si is its role in bodily sensation. Namely, Si monitors internal bodily affairs, ensuring that physical needs are optimally satisfied. Being an introverted function, Si is more intensive than Se is, which can make ISFJs more sensitive to a variety of sensory stimuli such as lighting, room temperature, noise levels, sleeping surfaces, etc. They can also be sensitive to strong flavors and unfamiliar textures, which is why they commonly prefer what Se types might consider a bland, simple, or routinized diet.

The bodily role of Si can also influence ISFJs' health. It may, for instance, allow them to be more attuned to when they are full, thereby preventing overeating. On the other hand, it could play a role in health problems, such as hypochondriasis, in which normal sensations become amplified and interpreted as signs of illness.

We can also compare Si with its intuitive cousin, Ni. As Perceiving functions, both can be viewed as functioning rather passively. Both can also be associated with a strong sense of conviction, which is why SJs and NJs alike can seem outwardly stubborn, opinionated, or closed-minded. The primary difference between these two functions is that Ni is a synthesizing function, producing its own impressions and interpretations. Si, by contrast, does not perceive a different reality behind sense data, but compares present experiences to past ones. For Ni, each experience is approached as new and interpreted on its own terms, whereas for Si, the past is granted a more prominent role.

While it can be easy for some types to criticize ISFJs for their conservative ways, we should not overlook their value and purpose. In addition to helping and teaching others (Fe), ISFJs help remind us of where we've been (Si) in order to prevent us from repeating our past mistakes. Si serves as a necessary cultural counterbalance to Se, reminding us that material resources are not unlimited and should be managed with care and wisdom.

ISFJs' Auxiliary Function: Extraverted Feeling (Fe)

ISFJs use Extraverted Feeling (Fe) as their auxiliary function. As the most interpersonal of all the functions, Fe is attuned to surveying and improving interpersonal feelings and morale. Like INFJs, ISFJs work to cultivate "good feelings" in the interpersonal environment. For the sake of surveying others' feelings, Fe helps ISFJs read emotional expressions and body language.

Interestingly, ISFJs may have a more difficult time with perceiving their own emotions than they do those of others. This is due to the fact that their Feeling function is directed outwardly (i.e., extraverted) rather than inwardly. Unlike ISFPs, whose Feeling function is introverted (Fi), ISFJs are less equipped to independently manage their emotions. Hence, when ISFJs find themselves in emotionally taxing circumstances, they often turn to others for support.

Fe also entails an extraversion of judgment. ISFJs utilize their Fe to express their thoughts, feelings, opinions, and grievances. Assuming they have not been severely censored in their upbringing, ISFJs are generally happy to share their feelings and perspectives.

ISFJs' Fe can present differently among strangers than it does with their intimates. In larger groups, they may seem characteristically "positive" in their expressions, as part of their attempt to cultivate good feelings. In the company of close confidants, however, they may be more open and direct with their concerns and grievances. In fact, self-expression a la their Fe is critical to their psychological and physical health and well-being. Even if doing so does not provide immediate solutions to the problem at hand, they tend to feel better once they have expressed their feelings, whether through words or tears. This is important for the mates or friends of ISFJs to recognize. While not necessarily looking for others to solve their problems, ISFJs value emotional support, empathy, and reassurance.

ISFJs' Tertiary Function: Introverted Feeling (Ti)

ISFJs use Introverted Thinking (Ti) as their tertiary function. Its role is to further refine their Fe judgments. It adds an element of logic that is less apparent in the early phases of their type development. Less developed ISFJs may draw very little from their Ti. Since their Si-Fe pairing provides them with strong convictions about truth, taking an additional step to Ti may seem unnecessary. With time and maturity, however, ISFJs can grow more comfortable with their

Ti and appreciate its inherent value. Ti can help ISFJs think more critically and analytically, serving as an aid and check to their Si-Fe process.

ISFJs' Inferior Function: Extraverted Intuition (Ne)

As is true of other types, ISFJs can be blinded to the degree to which their inferior function impacts their decisions and behavior. Without sufficient awareness and integration of their inferior, ISFJs will be prone to unwise decision-making in their lifestyle, careers, and relationships. Therefore, it behooves ISFJs to understand the ways their inferior function, Extraverted Intuition (Ne), manifests in their personality.

Ne is concerned with connecting ideas, brainstorming new theories, and conceiving options and possibilities. Prone to seeing connections and associations everywhere, it is an unpredictable and highly divergent function. This is why ENPs are often viewed as quirky, absent-minded creatives. While it is true that ISFJs can be routine and conservative, there are numerous ways in which Ne may manifest in their personality.

One way ISFJs may employ their Ne is finding creative ways to teach or engage with children. Since Ne might be construed as a rather "playful" function, there is part of the ISFJ that is childlike, that wants to play and let loose.

ISFJs may also employ their Ne through hobbies such as reading or word games. Many ISFJs enjoy working crosswords or other sorts of word puzzles. Such activities allow them to exercise their Si recall, while also making connections and associations (Ne). Many ISFJs also enjoy a variety of arts and crafts that allow for creative engagement of their Ne.

A less healthy means of engaging their Ne is gossip. By proffering speculations about people or events, ISFJs can obtain a quick ego boost for their Ne. ISFJs may also enjoy speculating about various religious or political topics.

Stock trading is yet another way ISFJs may engage their Ne. Since reading and analyzing market trends might be construed as an Ne-Ti endeavor, ISFJs who can successfully navigate the complexities of the market not only anticipate a financial reward, but a psychological kickback for their inferior function.

Like other types seeking to integrate their inferior function, ISFJs must learn that integration does not occur through direct use or development of their Ne. Instead, they are wise to allow their Ne to remain rather unconscious, functioning passively in the background. This allows them to focus their time and energy on what they do best (Si and Fe), trusting that integration will occur naturally as they consistently and authentically function as ISFJs.

ISTJ

Thought to comprise over 10% of the general population, ISTJ is among the most commonly encountered personality types, outnumbering INTJs at a clip of ten to one. ISTJs are among the most loyal, dutiful, and responsible of the types. They make loyal friends and companions and are admired for their devotion, steadfastness, and perseverance. If ESPs are the hares of the sixteen types, ISTJs are the tortoises. They work slowly and steadily until the job is done, fastidiously attending to all the details along the way.

In order to understand ISTJs, one must first understand their dominant function, Introverted Sensing (Si), which compels them to preserve and protect past ways of doing things. Their Si characteristics led David Keirsey to rightly describe them as "guardians." ISTJs guard and defend traditions and conventions, particularly those they have significant personal experience and familiarity with (e.g., their childhood religion).

Like ISFJs, ISTJs can grow attached to the routine and familiar. The more often they do something in a particular way, the harder it is for them to break out of that pattern. This not only applies to their behavioral habits, but also to their beliefs and worldview, as many ISTJs continue in the same belief system in which they were raised.

While ISTJs are at times viewed as stubborn or finicky, they are actually more easygoing than is typically accredited them. Since Si is a Perceiving function, their first preference is to assume a receptive rather than controlling attitude. Unfortunately, this often goes unnoticed, since Si is introverted in direction. This is especially true in work settings, where ISTJs are more apt to call on their auxiliary Te. Once away from the workplace, however, most ISTJs know how to be leisurely, something ESTJs can have a harder time with. In short, ISTJs are far less rigid and controlling (especially inwardly) than they are sometimes painted to be.

In sharing the same dominant and inferior functions, ISTJs have much in common with ISFJs. However, their auxiliary functions do confer significant differences. ISFJs use Extraverted Feeling (Fe) as their auxiliary function, which grants them a greater measure of social and emotional intelligence. And while ISTJs may lack some measure of social grace, their auxiliary Thinking function (Te) contributes stronger powers of logic and tactical intelligence.

Although differing in only one preference (i.e., J-P), ISTJs actually share zero functions with ISTPs. ISTPs, who use Se instead of Si, are less concerned with past precedent than ISTJs are. Their Se also confers a stronger desire for sensory and material novelty. Lastly, ISTPs are more inclined toward "hands-on" work, whereas ISTJ career-seekers are more disposed to administrative or other "white collar" sorts of work.

ISTJs' Functional Stack & Type Development

ISTJs' functional stack is composed of the following functions:

Dominant: Introverted Sensing (Si)

Auxiliary: Extraverted Thinking (Te)

Tertiary: Introverted Feeling (Fi)

Inferior: Extraverted Intuition (Ne)

ISTJs' personality type development can be broadly conceived as consisting of three phases:

Phase I (Childhood)

Phase I is characterized by the development and rise to power of their dominant function, Introverted Sensing (Si). ISTJs use their Si to absorb, integrate, and reflect on acquired information and personal experiences. Phase I ISTJs may also show some development of their auxiliary function, Extraverted Thinking (Te), which can serve as a helpful extraverted tool for navigating and managing the outside world.

Phase II (Adolescence-30s)

Once ISTJs' dominant Si reaches a certain threshold of consciousness and differentiation, their inferior function, Extraverted Intuition (Ne), begins to assert itself and play a more prominent and mischievous role. The tug-of-war between their Si and Ne will be discussed later in this profile. Phase II ISTJs also show increasing use and development of their Te and may even begin to tap into their tertiary function, Introverted Feeling (Fi).

Phase III (30s, 40s, & Beyond)

If all goes well and they are fortunate enough to enter Phase III, ISTJs become increasingly aware of the insidious ways of their inferior Si. As they become more aware of their inferior and learn to function more authentically as ISTJs, they experience greater balance between their Si and Ne. They learn that integrating their Ne happens naturally and indirectly as they go about authentically using their Si and Te. As they cultivate conditions that support their natural strengths, Phase

III ISTJs come to experience a heightened sense of peace, wholeness, and satisfaction.

ISTJs' Dominant Function: Introverted Sensing (Si)

As we've seen, ISTJs use Introverted Sensing (Si) as their dominant function. Si types (i.e., SJs) are quite different from Se types (i.e., SPs). Unlike SPs, ISTJs are not sensation-seekers. They do not venture out seeking novel sensations, experiences, or material goods. They typically prefer a more routine, careful (versus care*free*), and predictable lifestyle.

Si undergirds ISTJs' propensity to function as conservators of tradition. However, because Si is a Perceiving function, ISTJs are less inclined to function as frontline activists for their beliefs or values than ESJs are. Rather, ISTJs prefer spending time reflecting on the past and their cherished traditions. Many enjoy attending religious services or studying religious texts, activities that support and strengthen their Si convictions.

Another feature of Si is its role in bodily sensation. Namely, it serves to monitor internal bodily affairs, ensuring that bodily needs are satisfied. As an introverted function, Si is more intensive than Se is, which can make ISTJs more sensitive to certain sensory stimuli. They may be hypersensitive to things like lighting, room temperature, noise levels, etc. This can make them more irritable than other types when sleep-deprived, hungry, or otherwise physically uncomfortable. Sensitivity to strong or unusual flavors and textures may lead them to adopt a relatively bland or routine diet. Si can also play a role in problems like hypochondriasis, contributing to excessive attention to and concern for bodily sensations, so that normal sensations become amplified and interpreted as signs of illness.

We can also compare Si with its intuitive cousin, Ni. As Perceiving functions, both can be viewed as functioning rather passively. Both can also be associated with strength of conviction, as SJs and NJs alike can seem outwardly stubborn, opinionated, or closed-minded. The chief difference between these two functions is that Ni is a synthesizing function, weaving together disparate information to construct its own impressions or interpretations. Si, by contrast, does not see a different reality behind immediate sense data. Instead, it compares present experiences to past ones. For Ni, every experience is new and interpreted on its own terms. For Si, the past plays a more prominent role in interpreting the present.

While it can be easy for other types to criticize ISTJs for their conservative ways, we should not overlook their value and purpose. ISTJs remind us of where we've been and can thereby keep us from repeating our past mistakes. Their Si also serves as a necessary cultural counterbalance to Se, reminding us that material resources are limited and should be handled with care and concern.

ISTJs' Auxiliary Function: Extraverted Thinking (Te)

Extraverted Thinking (Te) serves as ISTJs' auxiliary function. It undergirds their tendency to outwardly express their judgments and opinions. ISTJs' tendency to "think out loud," by way of their Te, can be both a strength and a weakness.

On the one hand, their Te can make ISTJs strong and effective teachers or managers. On the other hand, it can result in them coming across as brusque, dogmatic, or controlling. Like other Judging types, ISTJs can be prone to overstating things or saying things that, in retrospect, they wish they could rescind or at least soften.

Unlike Extraverted Feeling, Te is not oriented to the preservation of social harmony. It is less personal and less attuned to others' feelings. ISTJs' preference for Te may therefore lead others to perceive them as lacking some degree of tact or empathy.

Te also strives to bring order, control, and rationality to external systems and operations. The modern world, characterized by a snowballing of bureaucracy and "red tape," might be viewed as an offspring of an unchecked Te. ISTJs' Te, in combination with their Si, makes them well-suited for administrative, clerical, and other careers that require careful attention to detail, protocols, and procedures. While other types may find highly structured work settings off-putting, ISTJs find them comforting, since they know what to expect and what their role is according to the delineated structure.

ISTJs' Tertiary Function: Introverted Feeling (Fi)

Introverted Feeling (Fi) is ISTJs' tertiary function. As an introverted function, Fi involves an inner focus on and analysis of personal feelings and values. Of all types, IFPs, who use Fi as their dominant function, are literally the most "self-focused" (in a neutral sense) with respect to their concern for independently exploring and managing their values and emotions. ISTJs, by contrast, whose Fi is far less conscious, do not always enjoy ready access to their own emotions.

As an inner Judging function, Fi grants IFPs a strong sense of inner self-control. But since ISTJs' Fi is in the tertiary position, they do not enjoy the same degree of inner control. To compensate, they, like other TJ types, focus more on shaping or controlling the outside world via their Te.

One of the more important features of Fi is its direction. Namely, because it is introverted, onlookers are often barred from accessing ISTJs' emotions. This is exacerbated by the fact that Fi is subordinated to Te in their functional stack. Consequently, ISTJs can appear cold, aloof, or unemotional.

As ISTJs tap into their Fi, they begin to attend more closely to their personal feelings and values, as well as those of others. They begin to recognize and appreciate the merit of subjective concerns, acknowledging that truth or value is not limited to past precedent (Si) or external standards (Te), but can also include individual preferences (Fi). In opening to their Fi, ISTJs can become more compassionate and understanding, even toward those at the other end of the political or religious spectrum.

ISTJs' Inferior Function: Extraverted Intuition (Ne)

As is true of other types, ISTJs can be blinded to the degree to which their inferior function impacts their decisions and behavior. Without sufficient awareness and integration of their inferior, ISTJs will be prone to unwise decision-making. Consequently, ISTJs seeking personal growth must work to understand the ways their inferior function, Extraverted Intuition (Ne), manifests in their personality.

Ne is concerned with generating and connecting ideas, as well as seeing all the various options and possibilities. Prone to seeing connections and associations everywhere, it is an unpredictable and highly divergent function. This is why Ne types are often viewed as quirky and unconventional creatives. While it is true that ISTJs are rather routine and conservative in their ways, there are numerous ways in which Ne can manifest in their personality.

One way ISTJs may indulge their Ne is through various sorts of speculation or prognostication. One of the most common ways ISTJs do this is through gossip. By proffering theories about various people or happenings, they secure an ego boost for their Ne. They also enjoy propagating various religious or political theories.

ISTJs also engage their Ne in their hobbies, such as word or math games. I know a number of ISTJs who enjoy working crosswords, Sudokus, or other sorts of puzzles. Such activities allow them to exercise their Si recall, utilize Te strategies, and make associations and experiment with possibilities (Ne). Many ISTJs also enjoy a variety of arts and crafts that allow for creative use of their Ne.

ISTJs also employ their Ne is by looking for creative ways to teach others. In addition to their desire to impart Si-Te information, creative use of their Ne may be another reason ISTJs gravitate toward teaching.

As for other types, integration for ISTJs does not occur through direct use or development of their inferior function. Rather, ISTJs are better off allowing their Ne to remain unconscious, functioning passively in the background. Instead of trying to develop or display more foresight, cleverness, or creativity, integrating ISTJs do what ISTJs do best, focusing their time and energy on Si and Te, while trusting that, in due time, everything else will fall into place.

ENFP

ENFPs are enthusiastic, idealistic, restless, and open-minded. They are among the most versatile of all types, working well with both people and ideas. As Extraverts, they are not opposed to action, while as Intuitives, they are not opposed to reflection. In this sense, ENFPs represent a sort of hybrid between Introverts and Extraverts.

ENFPs are novelty-seekers. They are constantly scanning for new and interesting people, ideas, and possibilities. Like INFPs, they enjoy abstract as well as more experiential forms of learning.

While seeking success in their careers and personal development, ENFPs generally take life less seriously than IP or EJ types (i.e., types with a dominant Judging function). At the end of the day, ENFPs want to have fun and may not be highly discriminating with regard to how that happens. Perhaps more than anything, ENFPs fear boredom and stagnation. Even sleep can seem a bit too boring or mundane for ENFPs.

The minds of ENFPs can move at a frenetic pace. They can be restless, anxious, and plagued by erratic sleeping patterns. As with ENTPs, one can even observe this restlessness in ENFPs' eyes, which are often darting broadly from one side to another, as though searching for something in their surroundings. What they are actually searching for, however, is more mental in nature, such as words, ideas, or possibilities (i.e., Ne). ENFPs are constantly generating new ideas, associations, and quips. They can often seem random, scattered, distracted, and flighty and, rightly or not, are commonly diagnosed with ADD or ADHD.

ENFPs are predominantly "right-brained" personality types. While the left side of the brain is concerned with order, control, and systematizing, the right brain is oriented to novelty, people, and emotions. The right brain is also the more random or "creative" side (i.e., divergence), while the left hemisphere is concerned with analysis and predictability (i.e., convergence).

ENFPs place high value on their personal experiences when it comes to discerning truth. Though not to the same extent as ESFPs, for ENFPs, "experiencing is believing." Because of the high value they place on their personal experiences, ENFPs may feel they cannot fully know themselves until they have tried just about everything (contrast this with INJs, who feel they know whether they will like something without needing to experience it). For this reason, ENFPs are quintessential seekers and dilettantes, wanting to experience as much of life and the world as is humanly possible. In many regards, the interests and aspirations of ENFPs are infinite. This can be nothing less than exhausting for those trying to stay apace with them.

ENFPs are among the least judgmental and most inclusive of all types, both inwardly and outwardly. Much like INFPs, they are champions of diversity and multiculturalism. Their Extraverted Intuition (Ne) allows them to readily see different points of view, while their Introverted Feeling (Fi) supplies a sense of empathy and respect for individuality.

ENFPs are also connoisseurs of and participants in the arts and culture. They are commonly drawn to all sorts of creative endeavors. In particular, they often enjoy music, drama, and photography. Those with sufficient mental focus can also make great writers, be it fiction or non-fiction. ENFPs are highly represented among journalists, excelling with both the written and spoken word.

Career-wise, ENFPs are often drawn to ministry, counseling, or teaching. They love seeing and cultivating potential in others. While some ENFPs are content with working largely with ideas, others seek to combine this with action and adventure. Such individuals may take up work as missionaries, tour guides, or diplomats. Others may try their hand at politics. ENFPs' inferior function, Introverted Sensing (Si), may contribute an interest in history that may add to the allure of religious, political, or journalistic work.

ENFPs' Functional Stack & Type Development

ENFPs' functional stack is composed of the following functions:

Dominant: Extraverted Intuition (Ne)

Auxiliary: Introverted Feeling (Fi)

Tertiary: Extraverted Thinking (Te)

Inferior: Introverted Sensing (Si)

ENFPs' type development can be roughly conceived according to three phases:

Phase I (Childhood)

Extending from early childhood into late adolescence, Phase I involves the emergence and differentiation of ENFPs' dominant function, Extraverted Intuition (Ne). While ENFPs are typically open-minded and curious throughout their lives, this becomes more apparent with the development of their Ne, which is among the most open-ended of the functions. Beyond the requirements of school, Phase I ENFPs are generally free to sit back and absorb the world without undue worry or concern. This grants their Ne ample time to form extensive connections and associations. Phase I ENFPs may further expand their horizons through things like reading, travel, the arts, engaging with people, etc.

Phase II (Adolescence-30s)

Once their Ne reaches a certain level of conscious and differentiation, ENFPs' inferior function, Introverted Sensing (Si), enters the picture and begins to play a more influential and often mischievous role. We will discuss this in greater depth later in this profile.

ENFPs also develop their auxiliary function, Introverted Feeling (Fi), in Phase II. Fi serves to refine and clarify their values, worldview, and identity. The process of "finding themselves" entails both inner (Fi) and outer (Ne) exploration. As ENFPs develop and utilize their Fi, they may also become more serious, focused, and intentional.

Phase III (30s, 40s, & Beyond)

If all goes well and they are fortunate enough to enter Phase III, ENFPs become increasingly aware of the insidious ways of their inferior Si. As they become more aware of their inferior and learn to function more authentically as ENFPs, they experience greater balance between their Ne and Si. They learn that integrating their Si happens naturally and indirectly as they go about authentically using their Ne and Fi. As they cultivate conditions that support their natural strengths, Phase III ENFPs come to experience a heightened sense of peace, wholeness, and satisfaction.

ENFPs' Dominant Function: Extraverted Intuition (Ne)

Extraverted Intuition (Ne) seeks outer novelty. At first glance, Se and Ne types can appear quite similar, as both ESPs and ENPs can be outwardly active, playful, or restless. Ne differs from Se, however, in that it is more concerned with seeking new ideas, connections, and possibilities than it is with seeking novel sensations.

Ne is an extraverted Perceiving function. It can function either perceptively or expressively. The verbal expression of Ne amounts to something like brainstorming aloud. When orating, ENFPs may not always seem to "have a point" as they randomly move from one idea to the next. Often times, the "point" is for ENFPs to find their way to a judgment (Fi), but this first requires them to explore multiple options by way of their Ne. While others may not trust the seemingly arbitrary and haphazard ways of Ne, ENFPs realize its value. They know that, in time, that truth or wisdom will reveal itself. Their only job is to express their Ne, trusting that it will lead them in the right direction. Granted, some ENFPs are much more coherent and polished in their expressions than others; much depends on the context of the conversation. In some instances, ENFPs call on their tertiary function, Extraverted Thinking (Te), which is not at all random, but more direct and to the point.

In its receptive role, Ne works to gather information. It does not merely gather overt information as Se does. Se is more straightforward, involving a direct apprehension of information through one or more of the primary senses. Ne is different in that it goes beyond or looks behind sense data. This allows ENFPs to discern otherwise hidden patterns, possibilities, and potentials. Their Ne is constantly scanning for relationships and patterns among facts and experiences. ENFPs commonly employ the receptive side of their Ne in activities such as reading, exploring the arts and culture, and conversing with others. They enjoy asking questions that allow them to gain insight or knowledge from others, making them good facilitators of conversation. ENFPs often hone and apply this talent in careers such as journalism.

As an extraverted function, Ne is more divergent and open-ended than its introverted cousin, Ni. Once Ni has done its work, INJs are more apt to feel there is a single correct solution. ENFPs, by contrast, are disposed to multiplying rather than reducing the number of options or possibilities.

ENFPs also use their Ne to sniff out intriguing possibilities. They enjoy the role of wanderer or seeker. They rarely know in advance precisely what they are seeking, which is partly why they find it so exhilarating. Ne entails a sense of blind anticipation and expectation, of not knowing who or what will manifest next in their life journey.

Extraverted Intuition can also be associated with open-mindedness. It helps ENFPs see truth on both sides of an issue without forming premature judgments or conclusions. Ne can also involve openness to alternative or Bohemian lifestyles, allowing ENFPs to consider things like going vegan or joining a commune.

Like ENTPs, ENFPs can have a sort of love-hate relationship with Ne. They like that it helps them stay open-minded and allows them to see the value of different options or perspectives. They also enjoy its sense of adventure, expectancy, and wonderment toward life's mysteries. But Ne also has its challenges, such as making it difficult for ENFPs to draw firm conclusions or feel confident about their decisions.

ENFPs' Auxiliary Function: Introverted Feeling (Fi)

Introverted Feeling (Fi) is the auxiliary function of both ENFPs and ESFPs. One of Fi's primary concerns is the development of a personalized worldview, independent of societal conventions, which can serve as a platform for self-understanding and decision-making.

Fi is quite similar to Introverted Thinking (Ti) in that it involves an ongoing process of building an inner worldview and approach to life. The primary difference is that Fi focuses more on personal tastes (i.e., "likes and dislikes") and moral judgments (i.e., "good and bad"), whereas Ti thinks more in terms of "reasonable and unreasonable," "logical or illogical." Consequently, ENFPs first inclination is to use Fi to make moral, artistic, or taste-related evaluations, whereas ENTPs use Ti to evaluate the validity and veracity of concepts.

The difference between Fi in ENFPs versus INFPs is its place in the functional stack. For INFPs, it comes first, which makes them quicker to judge. Afterward, they use their Ne to probe the judgment to see if it is valid or whether it should be kept open or "grey." For ENFPs, the order is reversed. They do not start with an initial judgment or presumption like INFPs. This is particularly true in Phase I of their development. ENPs are wired to approach each situation with the openness of their Ne. After exploring things by way of their Ne, they use their Fi to form a judgment. Then, if they feel confident in that judgment, they may express it through their tertiary Te.

One of the more important features of Fi is its direction. Namely, because it is introverted, outsiders may not have easy access to ENFPs' emotions, with the exception of their general spiritedness and enthusiasm. Like ESFPs, ENFPs express their Feeling judgments somewhat indirectly through their Te. This may at times lead others to view ENFPs as Thinking types, while seeing ENTPs, who extravert their judgments by way of Extraverted Feeling, as Feeling types.

ENFPs' Tertiary Function: Extraverted Thinking (Te)

Extraverted Thinking (Te) involves the outward expression of rational judgments and opinions. Since Te is ENFPs' preferred extraverted Judging function and falls lower in their functional stack, ENFPs are generally less comfortable extroverting judgments than keeping their judgments to themselves (Fi). This may lead them, along with other Perceiving types, to habitually defer to others' wishes rather than asserting their own. And since ENFPs have independent minds, they can grow resentful of those who try to control them. With that said, ENFPs tend to be somewhat more self-assertive than IPs, but their relative discomfort with utilizing their Te can still land them in relational trouble.

As with other Perceiving types, ENFPs can also disposed to passive-aggressive behavior, involving the expression of negative feelings in indirect and underhanded ways. For instance, an ENFP might suddenly discontinue correspondence with a friend after furtively feeling offended by something he said.

To improve their communication in relationships, ENFPs can develop the ability to confidently assert themselves through their Te. In hoping to live up to their ideal of authenticity, they can learn to express themselves more honestly and directly.

Self-actualizing ENFPs find a source of strength and confidence in their Te. They find the courage to stand-up for themselves, to overcome their fear that conflict or disharmony will necessitate a bad outcome. They come to see how forthright expression can enhance intimacy. Te can also contribute to ENFPs' leadership capacities.

ENFPs' Inferior Function: Introverted Sensing (Si)

As with other types, ENFPs can be blinded to the degree to which their inferior function impacts their decisions and behavior. Consequently, ENFPs seeking self-knowledge and personal growth must work to understand the ways their inferior function, Introverted Sensing (Si), manifests in their personality.

Si uses information from the past to inform the present. It is attuned to past ways of doing things, engendering a concern for preserving certain traditions and conventions. Si types (i.e., SJs) are creatures of routine and habit. In contrast to Se types, they have a diminished need for novel physical pleasures, lavish surroundings, or material comforts.

Si is best understood in juxtaposition with its functional opposite, Ne. Despite being opposites, when considered together, Ne and Si constitute a meaningful whole. As we've seen, Ne is concerned with exploring new ideas and possibilities. Si, in contrast, is focused on preserving the past. Ne knows no limits, seeing options and opportunities as endless, while Si sees clearly defined limits as determined by past precedent. Ne seeks the new and novel, Si the tried and true. Interestingly, all of these opposing forces can exist within the same personality type. ENFPs tend to consciously identify with the needs and values of their Ne, while their subconscious rallies for the values and desires associated with Si.

Mind (N) & Body (S)

A most overlooked feature of Si is its perception of internal bodily sensations—the body as felt and experienced from within. This element of Si becomes more evident during activities that direct attention to one's internal bodily state, such as meditation, yoga, or Tai-Chi.

Since Si is their inferior function, ENFPs can lack some degree of inner bodily awareness. In their attempts to compensate, they may grant too much attention to certain physical sensations. This can make them more susceptible to hypochondriasis or psychosomatic illnesses, in which a heightened focus on bodily sensations cultivates or amplifies physical symptoms. Because of the powerful role of the mind in both health and illness, negative imaginings may even promote the development of real physical problems and illnesses.

Big Picture (N) vs. Details (S); Perfectionism

When operating in Ne mode, ENFPs tend to be oblivious to details. They focus on abstract ideas and the big picture rather than details or minutia. They may struggle to effectively attend to the concrete details of daily life, such as forgetting to pay the bills, eating a poor diet, or failing to take enough exercise. When engrossed in a creative project, however, ENFPs can look like INFJs. They can become perfectionistic and obsessive over details. It can be hard for them to accept anything less than the perfect material embodiment (S) of their imagined design (N). Walt Disney and Steve Jobs, both of whom were ENPs, exemplified this N-S perfectionism.

Future (Ne) vs. Past (Si); Novel (Ne) vs. Traditional (Si)

Si concerns itself with the past, while Ne focuses on future options or possibilities. ENFPs' Si, combined with their tertiary Te, can take an interest in the facts and details of history. They may also enjoy using their Ne to explore historical meanings, as well as the implications of history's lessons for a better future. This is why many ENFPs and ENTPs turn to politics or journalism, careers that allow them to use their knowledge of history to analyze current events and speculate about the future.

ENFPs often experience a sense of tension between the familiar and traditional (Si) versus the novel and unconventional (Ne). This is especially common for ENFPs in their teens and twenties. At some level, ENFPs are attached and drawn to the traditions of their childhood (Si). On the other, their Ne and Fi may encourage them to reconsider those same traditions. This can contribute to identity confusion among ENFPs, finding themselves unsure of the degree to which they should break from their childhood traditions versus reinventing themselves.

ENFPs raised in strong religious families may even experience a sense of guilt in allowing their Ne to roam free. But they are also motivated by their inferior Si to fashion a life that is more predictable and routine than would be possible if their Ne went unchecked. Such struggles can leave ENFPs with questions like: Do I want to start a family or do I want to live a freer and less fettered lifestyle? Should I take a good-paying job in a conventional career (Si) or try my hand at something more creative and risky (Ne)?

In weighing such questions, ENFPs, like other types, are wise to ensure they are leading with their dominant function rather than their inferior. As Ne-dominants, ENFPs' signature strength is creative exploration. To best utilize their creativity, they need to ensure they are not allowing their Si to impose excessive limitations or boundaries on their explorations. ENFPs are typically better to use their Ne, as well as the reasoning capacities of their Fi, to hash out truth, rather than deferring to Si tradition. Their Si may however supply some of the raw material for their Ne and Fi to explore and analyze.

For example, an ENFP who leads with her Si might start with the conclusion that the religion of her youth is true. She might then use her Ne and Fi to further explore that religion, without really questioning whether she had the right starting point. In contrast, an ENFP leading with Ne would not start with the assumption that the religion is true. While she would include her Si experiences in exploring its merits, she would not allow religious dogmas to restrict or bias her initial analyses. Only after exploring all the options, a process that typically takes years, would her beliefs grow clearer and allow her to draw firmer conclusions regarding the teachings of her youth.

ENTP

ENTPs are versatile, open-minded, and restless. Easily bored, they are constantly toying with new ideas and scanning for possibilities. Because of their insatiable thirst for novelty, their interests can seem limitless.

As is true of ENFPs, ENTPs' minds move at a frenetic pace, contributing to restlessness, anxiousness, and erratic sleeping patterns. Not only are they constantly scanning for new possibilities, but also generating new ideas and associations. Moreover, ENTPs enjoy sharing and exchanging their ideas with others. Considering how their minds are drawn in so many different directions, it is no wonder that ENTPs can seem restless, scattered, distractible, and, rightly or not, are commonly diagnosed with ADD or ADHD.

Unlike ENTJs or other types with a dominant Judging function, ENTPs do not carefully screen and filter incoming information. They are truly among the most open-minded of all types when it comes to absorbing outside information. However, just because they are permeable to new information does not mean they are quick to accept it as true. As ENTPs ingest ideas over time, they gradually develop, even if somewhat passively, their own theories about the world and human nature. When these theories don't square with conventional thinking, which is often the case, they grow increasingly skeptical and critical of majority viewpoints. So despite their status as Extraverts,

ENTPs can resemble INT types with regard to their skepticism and unconventional thinking.

When engrossed in their dominant function, Extraverted Intuition (Ne), ENTPs are not highly intentional or agenda-driven (their only agenda might be one of avoiding boredom). Hence, they may not be as consciously driven or obsessed with hammering down truth as some INTPs are. Nonetheless, many ENTPs, especially those who have developed their auxiliary function, Introverted Thinking (Ti), come to recognize their penchant for philosophizing. Like INTPs, they enjoy exploring unifying patterns and broad metaphysical speculations. Despite these propensities, they seem less apt to develop an exclusive focus on intellectual pursuits. As Extraverts, they can be reluctant to focus on any singular pursuit, preferring to distribute their energies across different hobbies and interests.

ENTPs' tertiary function, Extraverted Feeling (Fe), is a strong interpersonal function. This, along with their verbose Ne, contributes to ENTPs' love for engaging with others possessing similar interests. Despite their tendency toward restlessness and distractibility, ENTPs can focus when partaking in stimulating discussions or activities. Like INTPs, they are more interested in discussing ideas than engaging in small talk. Their Ne, Ti, and Fe confer an interest in analyzing what makes people tick—their motivations, interests, patterns, and propensities. Engaging with others allows ENTPs to sharpen their theories of human nature and enjoy themselves along the way.

When it comes to schooling, the degree to which ENTPs feel engaged depends largely on the circumstances. Like other NTs, they generally excel in math and science. But as dominant Intuitives, they tend to have broad scholastic interests that extend into the arts and humanities. Their inferior function, Introverted Sensing (Si), may also contribute to an interest in history. As abstract learners, ENTPs are more apt to enjoy traditional schooling than ESTPs are. Teachers often appreciate their intelligence, creativity, and genuine intellectual curiosity. However, if the instructor or coursework fails to be stimulating, they can quickly become bored, restless, and tuned out. ENTPs are also notorious for procrastinating too long, sometimes producing work that fails to reflect their true capabilities.

ENTPs are often better at finding their place among people (Fe) than they are at identifying an ideal job in the system (Te). Their Ne (as well as their lack of Te) can make ENTPs reluctant to work within highly structured systems or organizations. Unfortunately, the modern working world seems primarily suited for those with Te in their functional stack (especially TJ types). Rife with rules, policies, and regulations, nearly all professions, as well as academic and research institutions, have become Te-laden in their methods and operations. Consequently, ENTPs often struggle to find jobs and careers that allow them to function authentically as ENTPs.

Career-wise, ENTPs are best suited for working with people and ideas. Since many ENTPs are effective writers and orators, they often do well as journalists, writers, or editors. While apt to grow weary of the increasing standardization and bureaucracy of the modern education system, ENTPs may also enjoy teaching. ENTPs with religious affiliations may function as missionaries, pastors, or ministers, although their knack for deviating from conventional dogmas and traditions may precipitate problems. ENTPs may also enjoy work as actors, mediators, diplomats, or entrepreneurs.

ENTPs' Functional Stack & Type Development

ENTPs' functional stack is composed of the following functions:

Dominant: Extraverted Intuition (Ne)

Auxiliary: Introverted Thinking (Ti)

Tertiary: Extraverted Feeling (Fe)

Inferior: Introverted Sensing (Si)

ENTPs' type development can be roughly divided according to three phases:

Phase I (Childhood)

Extending from childhood to early adulthood, Phase I involves the emergence and differentiation of the ENTPs' dominant function, Extraverted Intuition (Ne). While ENTPs are generally curious and open-minded throughout their lives, this is especially pronounced during this phase of their development. Beyond the requirements of schooling, Phase I ENTPs are free to sit back and absorb the world without undue worry or concern. This allows their Ne to make all sorts of connections and associations, which can eventually coalesce into a coherent worldview.

Phase II (Adolescence-30s)

Once their Ne reaches a certain level of consciousness and differentiation, ENTPs' inferior function, Introverted Sensing (Si), enters the picture and begins to play a more influential and often mischievous role. We will discuss ENTPs' inferior-function related issues later in this profile.

In addition to the increasing presence and influence of Si, Phase II ENTPs are also developing their auxiliary function, Introverted Thinking (Ti). Ti brings greater order and clarity to ENTPs' ideas, worldview, and identity. As ENTPs develop and utilize their Ti, they may also become more serious, focused, and driven.

Phase III (30s, 40s, & Beyond)

If all goes well and they are fortunate enough to enter Phase III, ENTPs become increasingly aware of the insidious ways of their inferior Si. As they become more aware of their inferior and learn to function more authentically as ENTPs, they experience greater balance between their Ne and Si. They learn that integrating their Si happens naturally and indirectly as they go about authentically using their Ne and Ti. As they cultivate conditions that support their natural strengths, Phase III ENTPs come to experience a heightened sense of peace, wholeness, and satisfaction.

ENTPs' Dominant Function: Extraverted Intuition (Ne)

As explained in *My True Type*, EPs are really "purer" Perceivers than IPs are. Not only do EPs display the outer characteristics commonly associated with Perceiving (e.g., spontaneous, adaptable, receptive), but their dominant function (Ne or Se) is also a Perceiving function.

Extraverted Intuition (Ne) is a novelty-seeking function. At first glance, Se and Ne types may seem fairly similar (such conflation can be seen, for instance, in the Enneagram Seven), since both ESPs and ENPs can be outwardly active, energetic, and playful. Ne differs from Se, however, in that it is more concerned with ideas, connections, and possibilities than it is with novel sensations or material goods.

Extraverted Intuition can function either perceptively or expressively. The verbal expression of Ne amounts to something like brainstorming aloud. Although typically not to the same extent as ENFPs, when orating aloud, ENTPs may not always seem to "have a point," quickly bouncing from one idea to the next. In many cases, "the point" is for ENTPs to find their way to a judgment, but they must first explore the options by way of their Ne. While others may distrust the seemingly arbitrary or haphazard ways of Ne, ENTPs realize its value, recognizing that in time, truth or wisdom will reveal itself. ENTPs' primary job then, is to employ and express their Ne, trusting that it will lead them in the right direction. With that said, some ENTPs are much more cogent and streamlined in their expressions than others. Many ENTPs learn to develop and express themselves via their tertiary function, Extraverted Feeling (Fe), which is not at all random, but more direct and coherent.

Ne also works receptively, gathering information from without. Unlike Se, it does not gather overt information, but goes beyond or looks behind sensory data. It is what allows ENTPs to discern otherwise hidden patterns, possibilities, and potentials. Ne is constantly scanning for new connections and patterns. They often employ this receptive side of their Ne in activities like reading, watching movies, and conversing with others.

Because it is an extraverted function, Ne is more divergent, extensive, and open-ended than Introverted Intuition (Ni). Ni is more intensive and convergent, conferring a greater sense of conviction and closure. Once Ni has done its work, INJs are apt to feel there is a single correct solution. Ne, by contrast, is disposed to multiplying rather than reducing the number of possible options or solutions. Only through use of their auxiliary Ti can ENTPs move toward convergence.

Ne also confers open-mindedness. It helps ENTPs see truth on both sides of an issue without forming unwarranted judgments or premature conclusions. It also contributes openness to alternative or Bohemian lifestyles, allowing ENTPs to entertain options such as vegetarianism or joining a commune.

Ne also resists excessive external structuring, which can feel like an imposition to ENTPs' sense of personal freedom and autonomy. ENTPs scoff at what they see as unnecessary or overly rigid rules, regulations, or procedures. They also dislike unchanging or sterile surroundings. When the environment is too bland or sterile, they can quickly become bored and restless.

Like other NPs, ENTPs can have a love-hate relationship with their Ne. They love the fact that it helps them remain open-minded, to see the bigger picture, and to appreciate different options and perspectives. They also enjoy its attendant sense of adventure, expectancy, and wonderment toward life's mysteries. But Ne also has its challenges. It can make it difficult for ENTPs to feel calm and satisfied, to arrive at firm conclusions, or to feel confident in their decision-making.

ENTPs' Auxiliary Function: Introverted Thinking (Ti)

As dominant Perceivers, ENTPs are disposed to taking a more passive approach to life, particularly with regard to the outside world. Like other EPs, they are content to remain in a mode of open Perceiving until they are prompted, whether inwardly or outwardly, to employ their auxiliary Judging function, Introverted Thinking (Ti). When ENTPs feel compelled to engage their Ti, they become more inwardly focused and intense, similar to the typical mode of operation for INTPs. But because Ti is introverted in its direction, onlookers may fail to notice this more rational side of the ENTP.

Ti involves the application of logic and reason for the sake of understanding a given situation, system, or problem. It also works to bring structure and order to the inner world. This inner structuring grants ENTPs a good sense of inner control.

When engaging their Ti, ENTPs dig into the background of their thoughts to better understand their origins and to ensure their ideas are logical. Like INTPs, they can quickly find inconsistencies or logical shortcomings in a given theory or argument. They excel at identifying exceptions or imagining scenarios in which the proposed explanation might breakdown. They find it easier to identify logical shortcomings or inconsistencies —to assert what is *not* true—than to confidently assert what is true.

The difference between Ti in ENTPs versus INTPs is its place in the functional stack. For INTPs, it comes first, which makes them quicker to inwardly judge. INTPs then use their auxiliary Ne to open up and further explore their initial judgments. In ENTPs, the order is reversed. Rather than starting with an initial judgment or presumption like INTPs, they approach things through the fresh eyes of Intuition. They then employ their Ti to analyze and enhance the logic and structuring of their Ne perceptions.

In addition to the different ordering of their functional stacks, ENTPs, as dominant Perceivers, can more easily leave things open-ended or ambiguous than INTPs can. Their Ne dominance also makes them more open to "playing" than INTPs are. I once administered a values inventory and was surprised when a couple ENTPs marked "having fun" as one of their top priorities in life. To most INTPs, whose dominant Ti compels them to take life seriously, such a response smacks of hedonism and would likely be among their lowest ranked values. ENTPs' dominant Ne may also confer a greater interest in the arts and culture than typically seen among INTPs.

The difference between Ti and Fi seems largely a matter of interests and emphases. Fi types (FPs) are more concerned and skilled with moral judgments (Fi) than logical ones (Ti). They judge in terms of good and bad, love and hate, like and dislike. TPs, in contrast, start out with a need for sound logic (Ti) and are generally less concerned with matters of taste or morality upfront. They think less in terms of love and hate than reasonable and unreasonable, logical and illogical. With that said, since T and F are adjacent in ENTPs' functional stack, it can sometimes be a bit tricky, especially early in their development, to tease out their T-F preference.

ENTPs' Tertiary Function: Extraverted Feeling (Fe)

ENTPs' tertiary function is Extraverted Feeling (Fe). Fe is the most interpersonal of all the functions, striving for interpersonal peace, harmony, and understanding. This not only involves attending to *what* is said, but also *how* something is said. While ENTPs may be less disturbed by or sensitive to external disharmony than some other types, they still work, even if largely unwittingly, to cultivate good feelings in the environment.

We can also approach ENTPs' Fe more theoretically. Namely, since Fe is their preferred extraverted Judging function and falls lower in their functional stack, ENTPs are less comfortable extroverting judgments (Fe) than keeping them to themselves (Ti). This can lead ENTPs, along with other Perceiving types, to habitually defer to others' wishes rather than asserting their own. And because ENTPs have strong minds, they may grow inwardly resentful of those they see as trying to control them. Granted, they are generally more self-assertive than IPs are, but their discomfort in deploying Fe can still get kindle problems in ENTPs' relationships.

ENTPs' Inferior Function: Introverted Sensing (Si)

As is true of other types, ENTPs can be easily blinded to the degree to which their inferior function impacts their decisions and behavior. ENTPs seeking self-knowledge and personal growth must work to understand the ways their inferior function, Introverted Sensing (Si), manifests in their personality.

Introverted Sensing is best understood when juxtaposed with its functional opposite, Ne. Despite their oppositional nature, when considered together, Ne and Si constitute a meaningful whole. As we have seen, Ne explores new ideas and possibilities. Si, by contrast, is concerned with preserving the past. Ne knows no limits, seeing infinite options and possibilities, while Si sees clearly defined limits as determined by past precedent. Ne is liberal and unfettered, Si conservative and careful. What is fascinating is that all of these opposing forces can exist within the same personality type. ENTPs tend to consciously identify with the needs and values of their Ne, while their subconscious pushes for the interests of Si.

When using Ne, ENTPs can be rather oblivious to details. They may fail to effectively attend to the concrete details of daily life, such as forgetting to pay the bills, being careless with their diet, or not taking enough exercise. When engrossed in a creative project, however, ENTPs can look like INTJs, becoming perfectionistic and obsessive over details. As N-dominants, it can be difficult for them to accept anything less than perfection when it comes to the physical embodiment (S) of their vision or ideas (N).

A most overlooked feature of Si is its perception and awareness of internal bodily sensations—the body as felt and experienced from within. But since Si is ENTPs' inferior function, they may feel out of touch with their inner body. To compensate, they may grant too much attention to certain physical sensations, making them more susceptible to hypochondriasis or psychosomatic illnesses, in which an increased focus on bodily sensations cultivates or heightens symptoms.

N and S also have a temporal element. Si concerns itself with the past, while Ne is focused on future possibilities and potentials. ENTPs' Si can confer an interest in the details of history. They also enjoy using their Ne to explore historical meanings, interpretations, and implications. This is why many ENTPs take up politics or journalism, careers that allow them to use their knowledge of history to analyze current events and speculate about the future.

ENTPs also experience tension between the traditional (Si) and the novel or unconventional (Ne). This is especially common for ENTPs in Phases I and II of their type development. To some degree, they remain attached and drawn to their childhood traditions (Si). At the same time, however, their Ne and Ti may encourage them to deconstruct and even rebel against those traditions. This can engender identity confusion in ENTPs, unsure of the degree to which they should break from their childhood traditions versus reconceiving themselves. Such struggles can leave ENTPs with questions like: Should I opt for family life or an unconventional lifestyle? Should I pursue the security of a conventional career (Si) or something more creative and potentially risky (Ne)?

In considering such questions, ENTPs, need to ensure they are leading with their dominant function rather than their inferior. As N-dominants, ENTPs' best strengths involve creatively exploring ideas, theories, and connections. To best utilize these strengths, they need to ensure they are not allowing their inferior Si to impose undue limits or boundaries on their explorations. They are generally better off using their Ne, as well as the reasoning capacities of their Ti, to hash out truth, rather than deferring to Si traditions.

ENFJ

ENFJs are among the rarest of the sixteen types, comprising only about 2-3% of the population. They are warm, engaging, charismatic, persuasive, and talkative. They are the kings and queens of the social realm, capable of quickly reading and establishing rapport with others. Because of their love for people and formidable social intelligence, ENFJs develop extensive networks of friends, acquaintances, and social connections; they are networkers *par excellence*. Just as ESPs seek a breadth of sensory experiences (Se), ENFJs enjoy extensive interactions with people (Fe).

Like INFJs, ENFJs excel when it comes to reading people, quickly assessing and mirroring their emotions, expressions, and body language. This grants ENFJs great insight into people, contributing to their effectiveness as teachers, counselors, managers, salespersons, etc.

ENFJs discover their people skills rather early in life. Indeed, their self-esteem and self-image develops in large part around their social prowess. With each new person they encounter and connect with, their self-concept and self-worth are reinforced. Over time, ENFJs gradually become aware of their power to influence and persuade others. At some point, they realize they can use their powers of persuasion to get nearly anything they want. From that point forward, they must wrestle with the degree to which they are willing to use their charm and charisma to achieve their goals. They can take an "end justifies the means" approach, manipulating and politicking their way to the top. Or, they can forgo the temptation of quick success and preserve their integrity.

While "working a crowd" or charming an audience is undoubtedly invigorating for ENFJs, their desire to engage with people goes beyond mere superficials. Their auxiliary function, Introverted Intuition (Ni), adds a degree of depth that is less apparent in their ESFJ counterparts. Like INFJs, ENFJs see it as their job to help others live more authentically, ethically, and healthily. Utilizing their insight into people, they can be quite effective at diagnosing problems and formulating solutions that spawn personal growth. And because ENFJs are the most convincing (even if a bit forceful) of all the personality types, others often respond well to their counsel.

Although ENFJs certainly want to help and support others, their reasons for doing so are not always entirely altruistic. After all, as Fe types, their own sense of self is inextricably interwoven with that of others. So while ENFJs genuinely want those they help to succeed, if those individuals end up failing, the ENFJ may come down hard on them. After all, failure on the part of their students can seem threatening to ENFJs' ability to self-actualize, since their students are extensions of themselves. Deep down, the ENFJ may feel that a "poor student" is a reflection of a "poor teacher."

Another element of ENFJs that cannot be overlooked is their desire for self-mastery. As we will discuss later, this pertains to their inferior function, Introverted Thinking (Ti), which compels them to be self-controlled, self-directed, and self-regulated. Unfortunately, like other types, ENFJs often overestimate the skill and development of their inferior. So while they may aspire to or even believe they have achieved self-mastery, they are typically far better at evaluating and managing others (Fe) than they are themselves (Ti).

In sum, ENFJs are driven by several things. They are invigorated by social novelty and networking with people. They are also motivated by personal excellence and self-mastery, including the sense of validation that comes from being esteemed and admired by others. Lastly, and perhaps most importantly, they strive to quicken the personal growth of others, which, in turn, fortifies their sense of purpose and self-worth.

ENFJs' Functional Stack & Type Development

ENFJs' functional stack is composed of the following functions:

Dominant: Extraverted Feeling (Fe)

Auxiliary: Introverted Intuition (Ni)

Tertiary: Extraverted Sensing (Se)

Inferior: Introverted Thinking (Ti)

ENFJs' personality type development can be broadly conceived as consisting of three phases:

Phase I (Childhood)

This phase is characterized by the emergence and differentiation of ENFJs' dominant function, Extraverted Feeling (Fe). In developing and strengthening their Fe, Phase I ENFJs can seem inflexible and opinionated, quick to make judgments and draw conclusions about the world. Since their judgments are not yet being weighed and balanced by their auxiliary Ni, they are prone to jump to conclusions.

Since Fe is a rational Judging function, ENFJs tend to take themselves and their lives quite seriously. Even from a relatively young age, ENFJs are self-disciplined and goal-oriented, striving for excellence in whatever they do. They can differ markedly from INFJs in this phase, whose dominant function (Ni) is a Perceiving function. Ni prompts INFJs to be more open and take life less seriously than Phase I ENFJs are wont to do. While both types utilize Fe, INFJs are more concerned with ingesting and digesting the world (Ni), while ENFJs are already working to change or control it (Fe).

Phase II (Adolescence-30s)

Once their Fe reaches a certain level of consciousness and differentiation, ENFJs' inferior function, Introverted Thinking (Ti), enters the picture and begins to play a more influential and often mischievous role. We will discuss ENFJs' Fe-Ti tug-of-war later in this profile.

In addition to the increasing presence and influence of their Ti, Phase II ENFJs are also developing their auxiliary function, Introverted Intuition (Ni). As they encounter complex problems and situations that call for greater patience and reflection, they turn to their Ni for assistance. In doing so, they become increasingly capable of grasping and incorporating the bigger picture (Ni) into their Fe Judging process. Ni insight may also compel them to rescind or revise some of their previous premature judgments.

Phase II ENFJs may also begin to differentiate and incorporate their tertiary function, Extraverted Sensing (Se). For ENFJs, Se represents a further relaxing and opening of their judgments. It helps them loosen their grip on life, tempering their need for constant outer control (Fe). As their Ni and Se develop, ENFJs take on more Perceiving qualities, displaying more openness, flexibility, and acceptance.

Phase III (30s, 40s, & Beyond)

If all goes well and they are fortunate enough to enter Phase III, ENFJs become increasingly aware of the insidious manifestations of their inferior Ti. By increasing their inferior awareness and learning to function more authentically as ENFJs, they experience greater balance between their Fe and Ti. They learn that integrating their Ti happens naturally and indirectly as they go about authentically using their Fe and softening its judgments and its need for control through their Ni and Se. As they cultivate conditions that support their natural strengths, Phase III ENFJs come to experience a heightened and enduring sense of peace, wholeness, and satisfaction.

ENFJs' Dominant Function: Extraverted Feeling (Fe)

Extraverted Feeling (Fe) is ENFJs' dominant and most preferred function. As a Judging function that is extraverted in its direction, ENFJs are considered Extraverted Judging types. In laypersons' terms, this means they are quick to outwardly express their feelings, opinions, and grievances. They Judge before they Perceive, speak before they listen. This can be both a strength and a weakness. On the one hand, it contributes to ENFJs' quick responsiveness and capacity for leadership. On the other, it can dispose ENFJs to judging too quickly or too severely.

Fe also imbues ENFJs with a propensity to control or otherwise influence other people. This desire for control should not immediately be considered "bad" or unhealthy. As we've seen, Judging is a viable and commonly used approach to navigating life. While ETJs are more quickly recognized as controlling commanders, ENFJs' Feeling preference makes their means of control more subtle and in some ways more effective. Because of their ability to read and understand people, ENFJs can quickly and intuitively discern the quickest and most effective route to influencing them. This often involves schmoozing through eloquent language packaged in Fe warmth and friendliness.

While ENFJs are subtle and smooth in the public sphere, those who work with or have a closer relationship them will eventually see their more controlling or judgmental side. While Fe involves a penchant for maintaining interpersonal harmony and good feeling, this can be trumped by its commensurate desire for outer control and assertiveness. ENFJs are in many ways wired to express their feeling judgments as soon as they come about. This is obviously of great importance for their intimates to understand, recognizing that what comes out of the ENFJ's mouth is often their first reaction, one they may later come to reverse upon further reflection (Ni). Unfortunately, parents and teachers often fail to understand this about their ENFJ children and end up stifling their Fe expressiveness. This most certainly produces great frustration and possibly even psychological harm in young ENFJs.

Fe also plays a prominent role in reading and empathizing with others' emotions. It helps ENFJs recreate another's emotion state within themselves, allowing them to feel what the other person is feeling. Interestingly, ENFJs have a more difficult time when it comes to perceiving and making sense of their own emotions. This is due to the fact that Fe is directed outwardly rather than inwardly. Unlike IFPs, ENFJs don't spend much time trying to independently sort out their emotions. Inwardly, they deal largely in the currency of Intuition (Ni). Hence, when ENFJs find themselves in emotionally troubling circumstances, they often (and should) turn to others for support or guidance. Expressing themselves through their Fe is critical to their psychological and physical health and well-being. Even if doing so does not provide them with an immediate solution to the problem at hand, they tend to feel better once they have expressed their feelings, be it through words or through tears.

Fe is more influenced by cultural norms and expectations than Fi is. Just as Extraverted Thinking (Te) involves collective methods for evaluating and ordering information (e.g., the scientific method), Fe entails socially accepted ways of engaging with people. For instance, ENFJs typically display ample warmth, friendliness, and congeniality in their interactions. While Fi types may disparage ENFJs as emotionally superficial or disingenuous, most ENFJs have good intentions of improving morale or finding consensus. Even their attempts to control or schmooze others may be rooted in a larger desire for peace, diplomacy, and mutual understanding.

Finally, the dominant position of their Fe, combined with their auxiliary Ni, makes ENFJs among the most consistently goal-oriented of all types. ENFJs tend to take themselves, their lives, and their endeavors quite seriously. To the casual onlooker, this may not always seem evident, since ENFJs spend so much of their time engaging with people. But for ENFJs, their interactions with people are a key part of their life's work. ENFJs are highly intentional and often have an agenda—to teach, motivate, unite, persuade, etc. If they see little opportunity to effectively execute their agenda, they can quickly become restless and move on to something different.

ENFJs' Auxiliary Function: Introverted Intuition (Ni)

As stated earlier, ENFJs Judge before they Perceive. In many cases, it is only after making an upfront judgment by way of their Fe that they open themselves to alternative perspectives presented by their auxiliary function, Introverted Intuition (Ni). They differ in this respect from INFJs, who use Ni first and are therefore slower to express an initial judgment. ENFJ-INFJ differences emerge in social contexts as well.

As Fe dominants, ENFJs are first and foremost concerned with shaping what is happening in the immediate social environment (Fe). They want to ensure that good feelings are maintained or to accomplish whatever social objective they have in mind (e.g., teaching, advising, motivating, etc.). For ENFJs, Ni concerns take a backseat to Fe.

INFJs, by contrast, are more concerned with obtaining an accurate perception of what is happening (Ni) than they are with accomplishing any specific social objective. If they are faced with the dilemma of stating truth versus saving face, INFJs are more inclined toward the former. ENFJs, by contrast, are more likely to take an "ends justifies the means" approach than INFJs are. In order to accomplish their J agenda, ENFJs may be willing to say or withhold things that would not sit right with INFJs. They may also be more willing to feign happiness. ENFJs might reason, even if unwittingly, that if good feelings can be cultivated out there (Fe), then a sense of inner happiness will likely emerge in due time.

All of this is not to say that INFJs are somehow more moral or upstanding than ENFJs. Rather, this discussion illustrates the importance of the relative ordering of the functions in the functional stack, which invariably influences a given type's priorities, motivations, and actions.

ENFJs' Tertiary Function: Extraverted Sensing (Se)

Extraverted Sensing (Se) serves as ENFJs' tertiary function. While Si involves an intensive connection to the remembered past, Se is more extensive and present-oriented. It amasses concrete details and sensory information from the environment by way of the five senses (i.e., sight, smell, touch, sound, and taste).

Unlike Si, Se is not content with the routine and familiar. Rather, it seeks sensory and material novelty. Se types love novel sensations and appearances, physical thrills, and material comforts. They are more liberal than Si types in their approach to and use of the material world.

Se can also be linked with a concern for beauty and aesthetics (especially in Feeling types). ENFJs often have refined tastes regarding their material surroundings, their physical appearance, as well as their palate. They commonly display a taste for the finer things in life—fine arts, food, music, culture, etc. Consequently, some ENFJs may be perceived as snobbish or uppity, taking themselves or their sophisticated tastes a bit too seriously.

ENFJs' Inferior Function: Introverted Thinking (Ti)

Like other types, ENFJs can be blind to the degree to which their inferior function impacts their decisions and behavior. Without sufficiently understanding their inferior function, Introverted Thinking (Ti), ENFJs will continue to feel incomplete and be prone to unhealthy decision-making in their careers, lifestyle, and relationships.

Like ITPs, EFJs can be seen as trying to find the right balance between their Ti and Fe, independence (Ti) and interdependence (Fe), self (Ti) and others (Fe). For ITPs, Ti is far more conscious than it is for EFJs. While ITPs may feel they have little control over or influence with regard to the outside world (Fe), the inner structuring granted by their Ti confers a strong sense of inner control. This allows them to independently manage and order their thoughts and experiences so as to better cope with a world they see as outside their control. ITPs also use their Ti powers of logic to discern their own truth.

Because their Ti is inferior, ENFJs don't enjoy the same sense of inner control that ITPs do. Nor do they experience the same aptitude or confidence in their ability to consciously wield logic. Just as feelings are slippery and elusive for ITPs, so it is with logic for ENFJs.

However elusive their Ti, ENFJs are still captivated by it (as all types are with their inferior). In many ways, Ti represents a source of wholeness and self-actualization for ENFJs. Since Ti and Fe comprise a functional whole, they intuitively realize the importance of integrating these two functions for them to feel whole and complete. Consequently, ENFJs can be seen as striving for a greater sense of inner control and logical competence (Ti), which is why they may exhibit some of the same interests or self-conceptions as INTPs.

For instance, ENFJs may conceive of themselves as highly logical, independent, and self-sufficient. They may extol the virtues of independent thought (Ti), lauding the value of "cognitive-behavioral" strategies. They may also fancy themselves as self-aware or self-taught.

When indulging their Ti, they may lose themselves in stacks of non-fiction books or journals. Their Ti may even impel them to take up formal study in subjects like mathematics, science, or philosophy. Some ENFJs may even consider themselves Introverts because of their Ti attraction to heady or intellectual topics.

But just as other types misinterpret or overestimate the skill and competence of their inferior function, so it goes with ENFJs. In truth, ENFJs are not as logical or independent in their thinking as they imagine themselves to be; the majority of their Thinking-related ideas are typically culled from without. Moreover, as Extraverts, ENFJs are far better at reading, understanding, and controlling others (Fe) than they are themselves; they are more "other-aware" (Fe) than "self-aware" (Ti).

Since ENFJs are ultimately unsure of the soundness of their own logic (Ti), they may unwittingly try to convince themselves through the act of convincing others. The more people they can convince that an idea is sound (Fe), the more confident they hope to feel about its veracity (Ti). But the truth is that most people are not nearly as convinced by the content of ENFJs' Thinking judgments as they are by their persuasive Fe packaging.

As we've seen, personal growth is more about utilizing our natural strengths and enhancing the conditions for functioning authentically according to our type than it is about directly developing or "improving" the inferior function. In this light, integrating ENFJs learn to regularly employ their Fe and Ni, while allowing the Ti endpoint to take care of itself. Rather than over-emphasizing their skills as independent logicians (Ti), for instance, ENFJs are better off focusing on their relationships and social networks (Fe). While it may sound paradoxical, the best way for ENFJs to self-actualize and discover themselves is through consistent engagement with other people. By helping others discover and actualize their potential, ENFJs move ever closer toward self-understanding and personal wholeness.

ESFJ

ESFJs are one of sixteen personality types. I have found ESFJs to be less common than demographic data sometimes suggests, especially among Caucasian females. In my experience, they are easily outnumbered by ESFPs, at least in the U.S.

ESFJs are warm, engaging, caring, loyal, dutiful, and hardworking. They are admired for their work ethic, perseverance, devotion, and steadfastness. They strive to practice what they preach, holding fast to their commitments and convictions. As predominant Judgers, they take their work, family, and social roles rather seriously.

ESFJs have strong interpersonal skills, capable of quickly establishing rapport with others. They are natural readers of people and their emotions, a trait which allows them to quickly relate to people. Because of their social intelligence and love for people, they often have a substantial network of friends, acquaintances, and social connections. Their people skills also contribute to their persuasiveness and prowess as salespersons.

While appearing outwardly confident and assertive, on the whole, ESFJs are no more inwardly sure of themselves than other types. Indeed, because their inner Judging function, Introverted Thinking (Ti), is inferior, ESFJs may feel they have relatively little *inner* control. Finding inner control elusive, they naturally turn their focus outwardly, hoping that achieving outer control will somehow bring them inner calm and security. Their primary means of achieving outer control is through Extraverted Feeling (Fe), which serves as their dominant function. By way of their Fe, ESFJs can befriend, persuade, and direct others. In so doing, ESFJs can reap the benefit of social support, as well as a sense of control and influence in the world of people.

ESFJs' auxiliary function, Introverted Sensing (Si), prompts them to keep one eye on the past and to preserve existing methods, traditions, and conventions. This is why David Keirsey classifies them as "guardians." This may partly explain why many ESFJs love teaching, a role that allows them to relay existing knowledge and wisdom to others.

In sharing the same set of functions, ESFJs often resemble ISFJs. One difference is ESFJs tend to more warm and engaging upfront, while ISFJs can be somewhat more socially anxious and take longer to warm-up. These two types also differ with regard to their inferior function issues, with ISFJs wrestling with Ne and ESFJs with Ti-related concerns.

ESFJs can also resemble ENFJs, since they share the same dominant and inferior function. Both types have strong social acumen and enjoy helping and supporting others. But because ENFJs use Ni as their auxiliary function, they are often more interested in theoretical or philosophical discussions than ESFJs are. On account of their Si, ESFJs tend to be more practical and traditional, whereas ENFJs are often less conventional in their approach.

While ESFJs differ from ESFPs by only one "preference" (i.e., J-P), they actually share no functions in common. This makes these two types far more different than is commonly recognized. ESFJs, whose Extraverted Judging function is dominant (Fe), tend to be more direct and firm in their assertions than is true of ESFPs, whose Extraverted Judging function is tertiary (Te). Moreover, because of their Se, ESFPs are more concerned with keeping up with current trends and fashions, as well as modifying their appearance accordingly. ESFJs, by contrast, whose Sensing is introverted (Si), tend to have a diminished concern for doing so. Of course, ESFJs raised with Se types may assimilate certain Se tendencies because their Si has learned to see them as normal.

ESFJs' Functional Stack & Type Development

ESFJs' functional stack is composed of the following functions:

Dominant: Extraverted Feeling (Fe)

Auxiliary: Introverted Sensing (Si)

Tertiary: Extraverted Intuition (Ne)

Inferior: Introverted Thinking (Ti)

ESFJs' personality type development can be broadly conceived according to three phases:

Phase I (Childhood)

Phase I is characterized by the development and differentiation of ESFJs' dominant function, Extraverted Feeling (Fe). In strengthening their Fe, Phase I ESFJs can seem inflexible and opinionated, quick to make judgments and draw conclusions about the world. Since their judgments are not yet being weighed and balanced by their auxiliary and tertiary functions, they are especially prone to jumping to conclusions.

Since Fe is a Judging function, ESFJs tend to take themselves and their lives quite seriously. Even from a relatively young age, they tend to strive for excellence in whatever they do. They can differ markedly from ISFJs in this phase, whose dominant function (Si) is a Perceiving function. This leads ISFJs to be more open and take life less seriously than Phase I ESFJs are wont to do. While both types utilize Fe, ISFJs are more concerned with perceiving the world (Si), while ESFJs are already working to change or control it (Fe).

Phase II (Adolescence-30s)

While the inferior function is not entirely dormant or inert in Phase I, the epic tug-of-war between the dominant and inferior does not come to the fore until Phase II. Once ESFJs' dominant Fe reaches a certain threshold of consciousness and differentiation, their inferior function, Introverted Thinking (Ti), begins to assert itself and play a more prominent and mischievous role. This will be elaborated later in this profile.

Phase II ESFJs also show increasing use and development of their auxiliary function, Introverted Sensing (Si), and may even begin to tap into their tertiary function, Extraverted Intuition (Ne). These Perceiving functions allow ESFJs to open and modify their Fe judgments, as well as to loosen their grip on life.

Phase III (30s, 40s, & Beyond)

If all goes well and they are fortunate enough to enter Phase III, ESFJs become increasingly aware of the insidious effects of their inferior Ti. By increasing their self-awareness and learning to function more authentically as ESFJs, they can negotiate a better balance between their Fe and Ti. As they cultivate conditions that support their natural strengths, Phase III ESFJs can experience a heightened and enduring sense of peace, wholeness, and satisfaction.

ESFJs' Dominant Function: Extraverted Feeling (Fe)

As we've seen, Extraverted Feeling (Fe) is ESFJs' dominant function. Since Fe is a Judging function that is extraverted in its direction, ESFJs are Extraverted Judging types, quick to express their feelings, opinions, and grievances. This can be both a strength and a weakness. On the one hand, it contributes to ESFJs' quick responsiveness and capacity for leadership. On the other, it can dispose them to judging prematurely or too severely.

Fe imbues ESFJs with a desire to control or otherwise influence others. Whereas Fi dominants (i.e., IFPs) seek control inwardly, Fe types do so outwardly. This desire for outer control should in no way be considered "bad" or unhealthy for ESFJs. As we've seen, Judging is a viable and commonly used means of navigating life. While ETJ types are often viewed as controlling commanders, ESFJs' Feeling preference makes their means of control more subtle and in some ways more effective. Because of their ability to read and relate to people, ESFJs can skillfully discern the most effective route to influencing them.

Another feature of Fe involves meeting the needs of others. ESFJs work to ensure that everyone is getting along and is well cared for. ESFJs are often conceived as self-sacrificing, deferring their own needs for the sake of the collective good. In their attempt to cultivate good feelings in the social environment, ESFJs typically put on a happy face, displaying ample warmth, friendliness, and congeniality in their interactions. While Fi types may at times consider overt Fe friendliness as somewhat disingenuous, most ESFJs do so with good intentions of improving morale or finding consensus.

ESFJs' Fe can present differently among strangers than it does with their intimates. In larger groups, ESFJs may seem consistently "positive" in their expressions as part of their attempt to cultivate good social feelings. In the company of close confidants, however, they are more apt to share their negative emotions and grievances. And because their words are often bathed in emotion, ESFJs can seem intense or dramatic in their expressions. While such expressions are commonly interpreted as "irrational" by Thinkers or Fi types, they are rational to the degree to which they accurately reflect the nature of the experienced emotion. In many instances, given sufficient time,

ESFJs will further refine or soften their initial Fe judgments as they move through the Perceiving functions of their functional stack.

In contrast to IFPs, ESFJs can have a more difficult time independently perceiving their own emotions. This is due to the fact that their Feeling function is extraverted rather than introverted. Consequently, ESFJs don't spend as much time trying to independently sort out their emotions. Inwardly, they deal largely in the currency of Si. So when ESFJs find themselves in emotionally troubling circumstances, they often (and should) turn to others for support or guidance. Expressing themselves through their Fe is critical to their psychological (and physical) health and well-being. Even if doing so does not provide them with an immediate solution to the problem at hand, they tend to feel better once they have expressed their feelings, be it through words or through tears. Unfortunately, parents and teachers often fail to understand this about their FJ children and may end up stifling their Fe expressions. At least in the U.S., Fi seems to be the most common and socially accepted way to handle emotions. ESFJ females, in particular, can feel misunderstood in a culture predominated by FP and TJ females.

The dominant position of their Fe also makes ESFJs a proactive and highly intentional type. ESFJs tend to take themselves, their lives, and their endeavors quite seriously. They are efficient and task-oriented, quickly moving from one thing to the next. To the casual onlooker, this may not always seem evident, since ESFJs spend much of their time engaging with people. But for ESFJs, their interactions with people are a substantive part of their life's work. Even with communing with others, ESFJs often have an agenda—to help, teach, unite, etc.

ESFJs' Auxiliary Function: Introverted Sensing (Si)

ESFJs use Introverted Sensing (Si) as their auxiliary function. Si contributes to ESFJs' propensity to function as conservators of the past. The more often Si types do something in a particular way the harder it is for them to break out of that pattern. The same can be said for their beliefs and worldview. As adults, ESFJs often continue in the beliefs and worldview of their youth, including matters of politics and religion. The longer they are immersed in particular set of circumstances, the more difficult it can be for them to open themselves to alternatives.

ESFJs' Tertiary Function: Extraverted Intuition (Ne)

Like Extraverted Sensing (Se), Extraverted Intuition (Ne) is a novelty-seeking function. Ne differs from Se, however, in that it is geared toward ideational rather than physical or sensory novelty. Ne types are more concerned with being creative, making connections, or exploring options than they are with experiencing sensory or material novelty.

Since Ne is in the lower half of ESFJs' functional stack, they often have a love-hate relationship with it. On the one hand, they may fancy themselves clever, witty, creative, or savvy. This can be seen, for instance, in their desire to generate creative solutions or conjure clever comments. ESFJs may also employ their Ne in a variety arts and crafts or work to find creative ways of helping or teaching others.

The "hate" part of ESFJs' relationship with their Ne can involve the way it injects uncertainty into their beliefs and worldview. ESFJs seek a firm and unambiguous worldview to base their lives on. And because abstract analysis is not their strong suit, wrestling with ideas that contradict their Si worldview can be unsettling.

ESFJs' Inferior Function: Introverted Thinking (Ti)

Like other types, ESFJs can be readily blinded to the degree to which their inferior function impacts their decisions and behavior. Without sufficiently understanding their inferior function, Introverted

Thinking (Ti), ESFJs will continue to feel incomplete and be prone to unhealthy decision-making in their careers, lifestyle, and relationships.

As with INTPs and ISTPs, the overarching project of EFJ types can be seen as an attempt to forge a balance between their Ti and Fe, between independence (Ti) and interdependence (Fe), between self (Ti) and others (Fe). The difference is, for ITPs, Ti is far more conscious. They use their Ti to consciously create and maintain inner structure and order. While ITPs' feel they have little control over others (Fe), their Ti confers a strong sense of inner control and self-regulation. It allows them to independently manage their thoughts and experiences so as to better cope with a world they see as outside their control. ITPs also use their own Ti powers of logic to discern what is true and reasonable.

Because Ti is inferior in their functional stack, ESFJs don't enjoy the same degree of inner control that ITPs do (just as ITPs don't experience the same sense of outer control as ESFJs). Nor do ESFJs experience the same confidence in wielding Ti logic. Just as feelings are slippery, elusive, and ephemeral for ITPs, so it is with logic for ESFJs. Despite its elusiveness, ESFJs remain forever captivated by and in pursuit of their Ti. They intuitively understand that Ti is somehow important in their quest for personal wholeness. Therefore, ESFJs can be seen as striving for a greater sense of inner control and logical competence (Ti), which may lead them to exhibit some of the same interests and self-conceptions as ITPs. They may, for instance, view themselves as highly logical, independent, and self-sufficient. They may extol the virtues of independent thought or laud the value of cognitively managing ones owns thoughts and feelings. They may also fancy themselves as highly self-aware or "self-taught."

ESFJs may indulge their Ti by pouring over non-fiction books, trying to prop up their desire for logical understanding. Their Ti may even impel them to take up formal study in subjects like math, science, or computer programming. Some ESFJs may go so far as to consider themselves Introverts because of their desire for inner control or obsession with being logical. But just as other personality types misinterpret or overestimate the skills and know-how of their inferior function, so it is with ESFJs.

In truth, as Extraverts, ESFJs are far better at understanding and helping others (Fe) than they are themselves; they are more "other-aware" (Fe) than "self-aware" (Ti). Moreover, ESFJs are not nearly as logical or independent in their thinking as they might imagine themselves to be. Often uncertain of their Ti, ESFJs may try to convince themselves, even if unwittingly, of the veracity of their judgments through the act of convincing others. The more people they can convince that their idea is sound (Fe), the more confident they can feel in its logical veracity. But most people are not as convinced by the content of ESFJs' Thinking judgments as they are by their persuasive Fe packaging. After all, it is primarily ESFJs' Fe know-how that makes them effective teachers or salespersons.

As I've described elsewhere, personal growth is more about utilizing our natural strengths and enhancing the conditions for functioning authentically according to our personality type than it is about directly developing or "improving" our inferior function. As we learn to function authentically, many of our inferior function related issues begin to take care of themselves.

In this vein, self-actualizing ESFJs can capitalize on their strengths of Fe and Si, while allowing their Ti concerns to resolve themselves. So rather than over-emphasizing their powers of logic and independence (Ti), ESFJs are better off allowing their self-identity to overlap with their relationships and social networks (Fe). Moreover, when it comes to self-help, ESFJs are wise to include others in the process (Fe) rather than attempting to manage their thoughts and emotions independently (Ti).

While the prospect of directly employing or identifying with their inferior Ti can at times be tempting, this does not represent a genuine path to wholeness for ESFJs. Foregoing this temptation requires trusting that their personal growth will occur primarily through regular use of their Fe and Si rather than trying to control Ti matters directly. By staying true to their most conscious and authentic selves (Fe and Si), ESFJs can move closer to an enduring sense of peace and wholeness.

ENTJ

ENTJs are born leaders. They are direct, assertive, and uninhibited. They can become frustrated and impatient when things don't unfold according to their expected plan or time frame, evoking notions of the "Type-A" personality. In the presence of ENTJs, others may feel they are somehow being hurried or rushed, that the ENTJ wants them to "cut to the chase."

Like ESTJs, ENTJs are firm, direct, and outwardly opinionated. At times, they may be seen as harsh, blunt, or insensitive. Despite outer confidence and imposing presence, they are, on the whole, no more inwardly secure nor sure of themselves than other types. In fact, because their inner Judging function (Fi) is inferior, they may feel they have relatively little *inner* control. Finding inner control elusive, they naturally turn their focus outwardly, hoping that achieving outer order and control will bring them inner calm and security. Of course, controlling the outside world is rarely an easy task, contributing to ENTJs' propensity for restlessness and hypervigilance.

Unlike ENFJs, ENTJs don't enjoy ready access to the interpersonal benefits conferred by Extraverted Feeling. Instead, they rely on their sense of humor, fueled by their auxiliary function, Introverted Intuition (Ni), to ingratiate themselves to others. ENTJs can be great showmen and storytellers. Undeterred by conflict or controversy (they actually like being seen as edgy or provocative), they like to push the envelope, which not infrequently results in someone feeling hurt or offended.

While ENTJs can be quite funny when the time is right, they are, on the whole, quite serious in the approach to life. Their dominant function, Extraverted Thinking (Te), confers a strong work orientation. As we will shortly explore in greater depth, Te seeks to impose order, rationality, and efficiency on the world and its operations. Therefore, like INTJs, ENTJs are often drawn to science, or can at least appreciate the value of its standardized methods. One of the hallmarks of Te is its need for everything to be clearly defined, measurable, and quantifiable. This, in combination with their love for strategy and competition, can make ENTJs formidable strategists and executives. ENTJs are commonly found among CEOs heading for-profit companies.

Wealth and social status can also be motivating factors for ENTJs. This can be seen as deriving, at least in part, from their tertiary function, Extraverted Sensing (Se). Despite their status as Intuitives, ENTJs love worldly things. They are not opposed to owning high-end homes or taking extravagant vacations, just as long as these things are written into the Te budget. So while ENTJs certainly like to work hard, they can also play hard.

ENTJs' Functional Stack & Type Development

ENTJs' functional stack is composed of the following functions:

Dominant: Extraverted Thinking (Te)

Auxiliary: Introverted Intuition (Ni)

Tertiary: Extraverted Sensing (Se)

Inferior: Introverted Feeling (Fi)

ENTJs' type development can be broadly conceived according to three phases:

Phase I (Childhood)

This phase is characterized by the emergence and differentiation of ENTJs' dominant function, Extraverted Thinking (Te). Even early in life, ENTJs are goal-oriented. They are ambitious and seek success in whatever they put their mind to. Taking their goals and responsibilities seriously, they typically do well in school and aren't afraid to assume leadership roles.

During this phase, ENTJs can seem particularly inflexible and opinionated. They are quick to make judgments and draw conclusions about the world. Since their Extraverted Thinking (Te) judgments are not yet being tempered by their auxiliary and tertiary Perceiving functions, they are especially prone to jump to conclusions.

Phase I ENTJs differ markedly from Phase I INTJs. Since INTJs dominant function (Ni) is a Perceiving function, they tend to be more passive and take life less seriously than ENTJs. In Phase I, INTJs are more concerned with ingesting and digesting the world (Ni), while ENTJs are already focused on shaping and manipulating it (Te).

Phase II (Adolescence-30s)

Once their Te reaches a certain level of consciousness and differentiation, ENTJs' inferior function, Introverted Feeling (Fi), enters the picture and begins to play a more influential and often mischievous role. This will be explored later in this profile.

In addition to the increasing presence and influence of Fi, Phase II ENTJs are also developing their auxiliary function, Introverted Intuition (Ni). As they encounter complex problems and situations that call for greater patience and reflection, they turn to their Ni for assistance. They work to better see and incorporate the bigger picture (Ni) into their Te Judging process. As they develop their ability to assume different perspectives and to grasp the bigger picture, they become somewhat slower to judge, displaying greater foresight and discernment in their decision-making.

Phase II ENTJs may also begin to differentiate and incorporate their tertiary function, Extraverted Sensing (Se). For ENTJs, Se represents a further relaxing and opening of their judgments. It helps them loosen their grip on life, tempering their need for constant outer control.

Phase III (30s, 40s, & Beyond)

If all goes well and they are fortunate enough to enter Phase III, ENTJs become increasingly aware of the insidious ways of their inferior Si. As they become more aware of their inferior and learn to function more authentically as ENTJs, they experience greater balance between their Te and Fi. They learn that integrating their Fi happens naturally and indirectly as they go about authentically using their Te and Ni. As they cultivate conditions that support their natural strengths, Phase III ENTJs come to experience a heightened sense of peace, wholeness, and satisfaction.

ENTJs' Dominant Function: Extraverted Thinking (Te)

Extraverted Thinking (Te) serves as ENTJs' dominant and most preferred function. It undergirds their tendency to quickly express their judgments and opinions, to literally think (i.e., make judgments, conclusions, decisions, etc.) aloud. ENTJs speak before they listen, Judge before they Perceive. This can be both a strength and a weakness. On the one hand, it can make them strong and courageous leaders, while on the other, it can contribute to their being abrasive or controlling. It can also dispose ENTJs to advancing premature judgments and assertions. They may say things that, in retrospect, they would prefer to rescind, soften, or further qualify.

As mentioned earlier, Te strives to impose order and rationality on external world. It is quantitative in nature, pushing for objective standards and measurable goals. Rarely vague or ambiguous, it insists on clearly defined policies, plans, and procedure. Although their auxiliary Ni may contribute some degree of openness, ENTJs still expect things to be done according to their Te plans and guidelines. After all, if too much leeway is granted, they feel the system will not function at their desired level of rationality and efficiency.

Te also contributes to ENTJs' work-orientation. As T-dominants, ENTJs are generally more serious and focused than they are relaxed or receptive. Even on days when they have no external obligations, they are quick to get to work on something. Like other types with a dominant Judging function, ENTJs are not good at relaxing and doing nothing.

ENTJs' Auxiliary Function: Introverted Intuition (Ni)

Like other Intuitives, ENTJs are future-oriented, always striving for something more. They are forward thinking and change-oriented, getting bored or restless when things seem too repetitive, straightforward, or mundane.

Instead of thinking of their Ni in terms of "intuition," which can sometimes have a feminine connotation, ENTJs may use terms like "instincts" or "going with their gut." Unlike Ne, which tends to generate more options than it does firm solutions, Ni confers a higher level of convergence and singularity. Hence, ENTJs, as well as other NJs, often feel confident that their Ni answers or insights are trustworthy and reliable.

Like INTJs, ENTJs are not only are they blessed with the ability to isolate and analyze specifics (Te), but can also maintain a clear vision of the whole system (Ni), including its hierarchical structure and the interrelations of its constituent parts. Their proficiency with seeing both the big picture (Ni) and its specifics (Te) makes ENTJs masters of strategy, analysis, and planning.

Not only does a well-developed Ni make ENTJs better visionaries, but it can also temper their propensity to jump to premature conclusions. ENTJs can use their Ni to explore alternative perspectives and avoid the tunnel vision that may result from exclusive use of Te. Using and developing their Ni represents an important part of their personal growth, helping to ensure that their Te judgments are rooted in a broader, more comprehensive understanding.

ENTJs' Tertiary Function: Extraverted Sensing (Se)

Extraverted Sensing (Se) is a sensual, instinctual, and appetitive function. Se types seek out novel sensations, physical thrills, and material comforts.

ENTJs can have a certain worldliness about them, enjoying novel sensations, experiences, and material acquisitions. They can be particular about the quality, appearance, and status of their homes and possessions. Like other NJs, they can be captivated by the finer things in life, including the allure and status of affluent lifestyles.

With that said, the fact remains that ENTJs are dominant Judgers, meaning that their Te work generally takes precedence over any Se concerns. So while ENTJs can enjoy Se goods and experiences, they may be slow to make time for them in their T-oriented schedule.

ENTJs' Inferior Function: Introverted Feeling (Fi)

As is true of other types, ENTJs can be blinded to the degree to which their inferior function impacts their decisions and behavior. Without adequate awareness of their inferior, they will continue to feel incomplete and be prone to unwise decision-making in their lifestyle, careers, and relationships. Consequently, ENTJs seeking self-knowledge and personal growth must work to understand the ways their inferior function, Introverted Feeling (Fi), manifests in their personality.

Fi involves an inner focus on personal feelings, tastes, and values. Of all types, IFPs are the most "self-focused" (in a neutral sense) with respect to their concern for exploring and managing their personal values and emotions. ENTJs, for whom Fi is inferior and largely unconscious, do not enjoy ready access to their personal feelings and values. As for other dominant Thinking types, emotions can be slippery and elusive for ENTJs. Therefore, in situations where a "socially appropriate" emotional response is warranted, ENTJs can feel quite uncomfortable, since their emotional experience is often relatively weak. They may then resort to using their Te to offer condolences, etc., which can sound a bit mechanical, terse, or otherwise inadequate in emotional situations. ENTJs may also develop strategies for repairing a bad situation, allowing them to escape the awkward task of emotionally supporting or connecting with others.

Fi is also concerned with the development of a system of personalized values and judgments, independent of societal conventions. This inner value system and personalized worldview grants IFPs a strong sense of inner confidence and control. ENTJs, by contrast, do not enjoy the same degree of inner confidence because of the inferior nature of their Fi. To compensate, they focus on managing and controlling the outside world. They instinctively sense that the best way of controlling themselves is through controlling their surroundings. This is precisely the opposite of the IFP approach. IFPs feel relatively powerless in their ability to control the outside world (Te) and respond by focusing on the one thing they can control—themselves (Fi).

With that being said, it would be wrong to assume that ENTJs' Fi is powerless or lacking in influence. While they may feel they experience relatively little conscious control over their Fi, it can still exert its influence through less conscious means. As I have written elsewhere, the inferior function can play a prominent role in informing and orienting the dominant function, influencing its values and objectives.

More specifically, ENTJs' Fi might compel them to work toward a cause that has personally affected them. For instance, an ENTJ whose parent died of a rare disease may decide to become a physician or medical researcher. Their Fi might also lead them to place greater importance on the role of children and family in their lives than one might expect from a dominant Thinking type. This is not to say, however, that it is a good thing for ENTJs to be ruled or overtaken by their Fi. To the contrary, ENTJs, not to mention society as a whole, are better served when they engage in work that capitalizes on their Te-Ni strengths.

It is also critical that ENTJs consider *how* they are using their Te. Like other dominant Judgers, ENTJs can be prone to a sense of urgency when it comes to making decisions or finishing tasks. This sense of urgency can lead to premature and erroneous judgments, lower quality work, and obsessive sorts of behavior. For instance, ENTJs may have in mind for what they want to accomplish on a given day, only to discover the project to be much larger than they originally conjectured. But since larger task poses a larger challenge, they may "take the bait" and see if they can still manage to finish it. One of the problems with doing so is it locks them into Judging mode, as any deviation into Perceiving would likely prevent them from achieving their goal in the specified time frame. It might also lead them to shut out other people, who are then viewed as intrusions or impediments to their objectives.

To function more healthily, ENTJs need to ensure they are spending adequate time Perceiving rather than racing to finish things. While acknowledging their desire to reach a point of closure, ENTJs can benefit from remaining open to alternatives, realizing that Perceiving infuses their life with texture and richness. It allows them to live more organically, rather than always clinging to a preset agenda. This is not to say that ENTJs should stop being ENTJs and transform into ENTPs, but involves finding the right balance between Judging and Perceiving.

ESTJ

ESTJ is another of our 16 personality types. While some estimates suggest ESTJs comprise upwards of 8% of the general population, my research and experience suggests them as less common than both ESTPs and ISTJs.

ESTJs are dutiful, hardworking, and task-oriented. Often possessing "Type-A" tendencies, they can become impatient and frustrated when things fail to unfold according to their expected plan or time frame. In the presence of ESTJs, one can sometimes feel like he is being hurried or rushed, that the ESTJ wants him to "cut to the chase."

ESTJs are also firm, direct, and opinionated. Their verbiage tends to be succinct and to the point. At times, others may view them as harsh, blunt, or insensitive. Despite appearing outwardly confident and assertive, they are, on the whole, no more inwardly secure nor sure of themselves than other types. In fact, because their inner Judging function (Fi) is inferior, they may feel they have relatively little *inner* control. Finding inner control elusive, they naturally turn their focus outwardly, hoping that achieving outer control will bring them inner calm and security. Of course, controlling the outside world is no small or easy task, contributing to ESTJs' propensity for restlessness and hypervigilance.

Among the most "left-brained" of all the types, ESTJs typically present as relatively serious folks. Unlike ENTJs, whose auxiliary Ni can go a long way in providing fun and entertainment for all, ESTJs' Si may offer little in terms of lightness or humor. Those with a more salient sense of humor generally rely on their tertiary function, Extraverted Intuition (Ne), for witty or clever remarks.

Like their ISTJ counterparts, ESTJs tend to keep one eye on the past (Si). They aim to protect and preserve past methods, traditions, and conventions. This is why David Keirsey classifies them as "guardians." They grow attached to the familiar and expected, often developing a reliable set of habits and routines. As such, ESTJs like to know what to expect, to "know the plan." Unlike EPs, who are stimulated by novelty and uncertainty, ESTJs can find uncertainty or ambiguity unsettling.

Like ENTJs, ESTJs often rise to positions of leadership. The primary difference, in this respect, is that ENTJs tend to be visionary leaders, which often carries them to the very top of the leadership ladder. ENTJs also prefer to make and modify their own rules. ESTJs by contrast, are not only willing to give orders, but are generally okay with working under pre-established rules, guidelines, and procedures. Consequently, they often serve as middle-level managers and supervisors.

While ESTJs differ from ESTPs by only one "preference" (i.e., J-P), they actually share *zero* functions in common. This makes these two types far more different than is commonly recognized. ESTJs, whose Extraverted Judging function is dominant Thinking (Te), tend to be blunter and unapologetic in their assertions than ESTPs, whose Extraverted Judging function is tertiary Feeling (Fe). ESTPs display a certain social ease and smoothness that is distinguishable from the blunt approach of ESTJs.

All in all, ESTJs are among the most loyal, dutiful, and responsible of all types. Like ESFJs, they are admired for their work ethic, perseverance, devotion, and steadfastness. They strive to practice what they preach, holding fast to their commitments and convictions. They make loyal friends and companions, especially for those who embrace a similar worldview and lifestyle.

ESTJs' Functional Stack & Type Development

ESTJs' functional stack is composed of the following functions:

Dominant: Extraverted Thinking (Te)

Auxiliary: Introverted Sensing (Si)

Tertiary: Extraverted Intuition (Ne)

Inferior: Introverted Feeling (Fi)

ESTJs' personality type development can be broadly conceived as consisting of three phases:

Phase I (Childhood)

This phase is characterized by the development and employment of ESTJs' dominant function, Extraverted Thinking (Te). In developing and strengthening their Te, Phase I ESTJs can seem particularly inflexible and opinionated, quick to make judgments and draw conclusions about the world. Since Te is a Judging function, they also tend to take themselves and their lives rather seriously. While often perceived as outspoken or opinionated, Phase I ESTJs are developing the Te skills necessary to function as leaders and managers.

Phase II (Adolescence-30s)

While the inferior function is not entirely dormant or inert in Phase I, the epic tug-of-war between the dominant and inferior does not come to the fore until Phase II. Once ESTJs' dominant Te reaches a certain threshold of strength and dominance, their inferior function, Introverted Feeling (Fi), begins to assert itself and play a more prominent and mischievous role.

Phase II ESTJs also show increasing use and development of their auxiliary function, Introverted Sensing (Si), and may even begin to tap into their tertiary function, Extraverted Intuition (Ne). These Perceiving functions allow ESTJs to open and modify their Te judgments, helping them loosen their grip on life and temper their Te drive for outer order and control.

Phase III (30s, 40s, & Beyond)

If all goes well and they are fortunate enough to enter Phase III, ESTJs become increasingly aware of the insidious ways of their inferior Fi. As they become more aware of their inferior and learn to function more healthily as ESTJs, they experience greater balance between their Te and Fi, as well as an increasing sense of peace and wholeness.

ESTJs' Dominant Function: Extraverted Thinking (Te)

There are two varieties of Thinking: Introverted Thinking (Ti) and Extraverted Thinking (Te). The latter serves as ESTJs' dominant and most preferred function.

Te strives to bring order, control, and rationality to the systems and operations of the outside world. It is oriented toward quantification, insisting on objective standards and measurable goals. It carefully spells out how to get from here to there, using as many maps, directions, and labels as appropriate.

Te undergirds ESTJs' tendency to quickly express their judgments and opinion, to literally think (i.e., make judgments, conclusions, and decisions) aloud. ESTJs Judge before they Perceive, speak before they listen. This can be both a strength and a weakness. On the one hand, it can make them strong and courageous leaders. On the other, it can cause them to seem abrasive, dogmatic, or controlling.

Having a dominant Te can also make ESTJs prone to overstating things. They may say things that, in retrospect, they wish they could rescind, or at least soften. This is especially true for ESTJs with a hypersensitive inferior function (Fi), which can lead them to respond defensively or reactively.

As a Judging function, Te also contributes to ESTJs' work-orientation. Like other types with a dominant Judging function, they are generally more serious and focused than relaxed or receptive. Even on days when they have no obligations, they are quick to get to work on something. Even in their leisure time, they can experience a sense of urgency or hurriedness in getting things done.

ESTJs' Auxiliary Function: Introverted Sensing (Si)

ESTJs use Introverted Sensing (Si) as their auxiliary function. Unlike Extraverted Sensing types (SPs), ESTJs are less concerned with seeking novel sensory stimulation or acquiring new material goods. Instead, their Si prefers a more routine and predictable lifestyle. When combined with Te, Si also contributes to a sense of conviction about their beliefs and lifestyle, which is why ESTJs are sometimes perceived as stubborn or closed-minded.

Like other SJ types, ESTJs function as conservators of the past. The more often they do something in a particular way, the harder it is for them to break out of that pattern. The same can be said of their beliefs and worldview. As adults, they often continue in the beliefs and worldview of their youth, including matters of politics and religion. The longer they are immersed in particular set of circumstances, the harder it is for them to be open to alternatives.

ESTJs' Tertiary Function: Extraverted Intuition (Ne)

Ne is a novelty-seeking function. Ne differs from Se, however, in that it is geared toward ideas rather than the material or sensory world. Ne types are more concerned with being creative, making connections, developing new theories, or seeing new possibilities than they are with sensory or material novelty.

Since Ne is in the lower half of ESTJs' functional stack, they often have a love-hate relationship with it. On the one hand, it may inspire them to view themselves as witty, clever, creative, or savvy. This can be seen, for instance, in their desire to conjure clever comments or generate creative options or possibilities. They may also draw on their Ne for the sake of creative business or entrepreneurial enterprises.

What ESTJs may dislike about their Ne is its tendency to inject uncertainty into their beliefs and worldview. After all, ESTJs seek a clear and unambiguous worldview to base their lives on. And since abstract analysis is not necessarily their strong suit, ideas that contradict their Si worldview can be unsettling. In response, they may try to close off their Ne to various sources or ideas that they perceive as potential threats to their belief system.

ESTJs' Inferior Function: Introverted Feeling (Fi)

As is true of other types, ESTJs can be blinded to the degree to which their inferior function impacts their decisions and behavior. Without sufficient awareness and integration of their inferior, they will continue to feel incomplete and be prone to unwise decision-making in their lifestyle, careers, and relationships. Consequently, ESTJs seeking self-knowledge and personal growth must work to understand the ways their inferior function, Introverted Feeling (Fi), manifests in their personality.

As an introverted function, Fi involves an inner focus on personal feelings and values. Of all types, IFPs are literally the most "self-focused" (in a neutral sense) with respect to their concern for independently exploring and managing their values and emotions. ESTJs, by contrast, whose Fi is inferior and largely unconscious, do not enjoy ready access to their own emotions. As for ITPs, emotions, for ESTJs, are slippery and elusive, often taking an all-or-nothing character.

For IFPs, Fi also confers a strong sense of inner control. However, because Fi is inferior in ESTJs, they do not enjoy the same luxury of inner control. To compensate, they spend much of their time vigorously working to control the outside world. They instinctively sense that the only way they can feel in control of themselves is by taking control of their surroundings. This is precisely the opposite of the IFP approach. IFPs feel relatively powerless in their ability to control the outside world (Te) and respond by focusing on the one thing they feel they can control—themselves (Fi).

With that said, it would be wrong to assume that ESTJs' Fi is powerless or lacking in influence. While they may feel they have little conscious control of their Fi, it can still exert its influence through less conscious means. As I have written elsewhere, the inferior function can play a prominent role in informing, motivating, and orienting the dominant function, influencing its goals, interests, and values.

For ESTJs, their choice of work is often informed and motivated by the less conscious feelings and values of their Fi. This may lead them to take up work that deviates from what one might imagine for an ESTJ. They may, for instance, be driven by their Fi to take up work in ministry. While ESTJs are not innately gifted in matters of N or F (ministry might be roughly construed as an NF career), their move toward psychological wholeness does entail a reconciliation of their Fi and Ne functions. So while I am not suggesting that ESTJs are well-suited to function as ministers, we can at least understand why they might feel compelled to do so.

Fi might also inspire ESTJs to take up causes that have personally affected them. For instance, an ESTJ whose parent died of a rare disease may decide to become a physician or medical researcher.

Another example of Fi influence would be an ESTJ who opts to function as a stay-at-home parent. IFPs seem to have a particular empathy and concern for children, often finding great fulfillment in having and caring for children. Since ESTJs have Fi in their stack, they may have similar proclivities, even if far less conscious. Therefore, ESTJs may experience a sort of "high" from having or caring for children, even if doing so ultimately proves taxing or unsatisfying.

Personal Growth for ESTJs

As I have written elsewhere, we prepare the grounds for personal growth and personality type development by functioning authentically according to our personality type. This includes considering whether our circumstances (i.e., work, relationships, and lifestyle) allow for regular use of our dominant and auxiliary functions. In this case of ESTJs, this would involve regularly employing their Te and Si.

It is also important for ESTJs to consider *how* they are using their Te. Like other types with a dominant Judging function, ESTJs are prone to a sense of urgency when it comes to finishing tasks or making decisions. This often leads them to jump between their two Judging functions (Te & Fi) while spending too little time Perceiving (Si). Their concern for "being productive" can prevent them from absorbing or appreciating life (i.e., Perceiving); they may take their lives, as well as themselves, too seriously. While ESTJs are naturally disciplined and thorough, this can mutate into obsessiveness or compulsiveness if they aren't careful.

In short, personal growth for ESTJs occurs primarily through consistent and balanced use of their Te and Si. By staying true to their most conscious selves, they can move ever closer to an enduring sense of peace and wholeness.

ESFP

ESFP is another of our 16 personality types. It is among the most commonly encountered personality types, especially among women, comprising upwards of 10% of the general population.

Like ISFPs, ESFPs are often considered physically attractive. Of course, this might be partly attributable to their extraverted personality, as well as their concern for keeping up their appearance. They are attuned to what is trendy and popular, willing to modify their appearance accordingly. Glitz, glamor, perfume, jewelry—all are a part of the ESFPs' repertoire.

It's not that ESFPs are necessarily snobbish or narcissistic about their appearance. Rather, because of their dominant function, Extraverted Sensing (Se), they seem to have a natural eye for beauty, style, and aesthetics. Their homes are often immaculate and tastefully adorned, as ESFPs love to ensconce themselves in beautiful and well-accoutered surroundings.

As much as anything else, ESFPs are disposed to seeking sensory, material, and experiential novelty (Se). This is part of the reason they enjoy keeping up with current trends and fashions. Their Se is hungry for new stimulation—new sights, sounds, tastes, and experiences.

Like ESTPs, ESFPs also display high levels of kinesthetic intelligence. They are often athletic and endowed with good dexterity and hand-eye coordination. In contrast to ENFPs, who exhibit a preponderance of mental energy, ESFPs can display great physical energy. ENFPs use their Ne to explore new ideas. ESFPs employ their senses to explore and manipulate the physical world (Se).

ESFPs can also make great performers. Their sense of style and presentation, combined with their kinesthetic capacities, allow them to excel as actors, vocalists, and the like. For similar reasons, ESFPs can make skilled marketers and salespersons.

ESFPs' penchant for sensory and material novelties, as well as their knack for social "performance," has at times earned them the label of "hedonist" or "life of the party." While this may be true in some cases, especially early in their development, it only captures one aspect of the ESFP, namely, that of their dominant function (Se). What is often missed is the fact that many ESFPs present as intelligent, articulate, and composed. They use their tertiary function, Extraverted Thinking (Te), to express themselves in a measured and rational way.

ESFPs are generally adaptable and open to new experiences. Despite their status as Extraverts, they, like other SP types, are often more interested in "doing" or being otherwise entertained than they are in sitting around talking. While they can certainly be chatty at times, Se, by nature, is not a highly verbal function. ESFPs often express themselves through action rather than words, showing their love and thoughtfulness through gifts or acts of kindness.

ESFPs are often most verbally engaged when granted an opportunity to proffer advice. Rightly or not, they often see themselves as wise counselors. Because of their Ni function, they feel they can independently generate insights and answers for others' problems. This is why ESFPs often score as Enneagram Twos (i.e., "The Helper") and choose careers like counseling. Because Ni and Te make-up their subconscious ego, there may be nothing more ego-gratifying for ESFPs than giving advice. Wittingly or not, a common reason they maintain a wide social circle is because it provides them ample opportunity to advise others. ESFPs like having others turn to them for help and guidance, since it helps them feel valuable and important (it also gives their inferior Ni quite an ego boost). If they aren't careful, however, ESFPs propensity to proffer unsolicited advice can be off-putting to others.

Because of composed and measured presentation of Te, as well as their penchant for maintaining neat and tidy surroundings (even if largely for aesthetic reasons), ESFPs are commonly mistyped as ESFJs. In my experience, however, ESFPs are far more common than ESFJs are, at least in the U.S. As Si types, ESFJs are generally less stylish and image conscious than ESFPs are. And because ESFJs use Extraverted Feeling, they have a more natural sense of warmth and approachability.

While not to quite the same extent as ISFPs, ESFPs are lovers, nurturers, and caregivers. They love children and animals, whose relative helplessness makes them perfect recipients of ESFPs' affection.

Although ESFPs can present as warm and inviting, this is best understood as Se social performance rather than a natural expression of feeling. The natural direction of their Feeling is inward (i.e., Introverted Feeling (Fi)). Fi prompts ESFPs to manage their emotions on a largely independent basis. The sense of emotional independence conferred by Fi may also contribute to their confidence in advising others about how to manage their emotional concerns.

All in all, ESFPs are fun, active, attractive, and impressive. While generally fun-loving and easy-going (Se), they can also be assertive, controlling, and subtly manipulative. Like other personality types, their degree of psychological health depends on their degree of personal growth, including the way they go about reconciling their conscious and less conscious personality functions.

ESFPs' Functional Stack & Type Development

ESFPs' functional stack is composed of the following functions:

Dominant: Extraverted Sensing (Se)

Auxiliary: Introverted Feeling (Fi)

Tertiary: Extraverted Thinking (Te)

Inferior: Introverted Intuition (Ni)

ESFPs' personality type development can be broadly conceived according to three phases:

Phase I (Childhood)

This phase of development is characterized by the emergence of Extraverted Sensing (Se) as ESFPs' dominant personality function. Phase I ESFPs are fun-loving and free-spirited. They enjoy being active and drinking in all the experiences life has to offer. Since their foremost concern is absorbing and experiencing the world, Phase I ESFPs tend not to take themselves or life itself too seriously.

Phase II (Adolescence-30s)

While the inferior function is not entirely dormant or inert in Phase I, the epic tug-of-war between the dominant and inferior does not come to the fore until Phase II. Once ESFPs' dominant Se reaches a certain threshold of strength and dominance, their inferior function, Introverted Intuition (Ni), begins to assert itself and play a more significant and mischievous role. This will be discussed later in this profile. Phase II ESFPs also show increasing use and development of their auxiliary function, Introverted Feeling (Fi), and may even begin to tap into their tertiary function, Extraverted Thinking (Te).

Phase III (30s, 40s, & Beyond)

If all goes well and they are fortunate enough to enter Phase III, ESFPs become increasingly aware of the insidious ways of their inferior Ni. As they become more aware of their inferior and learn to function more authentically as ESFPs, they experience greater balance between their Ne and Si. They learn that integrating their Ni happens naturally and indirectly as they go about authentically using their Se and Fi. As they cultivate conditions that support their natural strengths, Phase III ESFPs come to experience a heightened sense of peace, wholeness, and satisfaction.

ESFPs' Dominant Function: Extraverted Sensing (Se)

There are two varieties of Sensing: Introverted Sensing (Si) and Extraverted Sensing (Se). Si involves a strong attachment to past precedent—to the routine, familiar, and predictable. Not only does it seek to conserve past precedent, but it is also conservative with respect to the material world. Si types (SJs and NPs) are less apt to lather on make-up or concern themselves with current styles and fashions, opting for a more "natural," simple, and less embellished appearance.

Se involves the perception of information through the five senses (i.e., sight, smell, touch, sound, and taste). It is sensual, instinctual, and appetitive. Compared to Si, it is more liberal and novelty-oriented with respect to sensations and the material world. Se types love novel sensations, physical thrills, and material comforts. They are "sensation-seekers," relishing novel experiences and the thrill of action. Many enjoy cooking and experimenting with new recipes. Because Se is concerned with "here and now" experiences, it can also be associated with a present temporal orientation.

Se attunes to the concrete details and sense data. ESFPs naturally scan the environment for interesting sensory novelties, noticing details that other types might miss. This is why they often have a strong visual recall, or what is sometimes dubbed a "photographic" memory.

Like other SPs types, ESFPs enjoy an array of sports and other "hands-on" activities. They commonly take up work as chefs, cosmetologists, nurses, waitresses, physical/ occupational therapists, and the like.

ESFPs' Auxiliary Function: Introverted Feeling (Fi)

Because ESFPs' auxiliary function, Introverted Feeling (Fi), is one of inner Judging, they are more serious inwardly than they might appear outwardly. Their Fi grants them a good sense of inner control, independently managing and regulating their emotions.

Compared to Extraverted Feeling (Fe), Fi is more individualistic and idiosyncratic. Because Fi judgments are formed largely independently, Fi types can be a bit wary of Fe expressions. To FP types, Fe can seem generic, fake, or contrived. With that said, since ESFPs often use their Se to mimic Fe, they are apt to be less bothered by Fe expressions than IFPs might be.

Rightly or wrongly, Fi can also seem more emotionally "mature" than Fe. This Since ESFPs' emotions are often repackaged and expressed via their tertiary Te, they can often come across as measured and rational; they may even be mistaken for Thinking types. Unlike Fe emotion, Fi emotion is not given an opportunity to "run rampant" in its outward expression–it is restrained. The same introverted property which provides such restraint is also responsible for its intensiveness. At times, that Fi intensity of emotion comes out through Te in the form of biting or sarcastic remarks, something ESFPs need to be wary of.

ESFPs' Tertiary Function: Extraverted Thinking (Te)

Extraverted Thinking (Te) involves the outward expression of rational judgments. As we've seen, Te contributes to ESFPs' ability to communicate in a measured and articulate fashion. Their Te is particularly active when proffering advice, at times leading them to seem preachy or condescending.

But because Te is in the bottom half of their functional stack, ESFPs are not always comfortable expressing their judgments, especially early in their development. This can lead them, along with other Perceiving types, to merely adapt rather than assert themselves. And since Perceivers are generally uncomfortable with direct conflict, they often mistake relational *harmony* for relational *health*, forgoing open communication in favor of preserving outer peace. So while ESFPs are generally more self-assertive than IPs are, those who fail to self-express via their Te can still find themselves in relational trouble because of inadequate communication.

Te can also inspire ESFPs to "be responsible," follow the rules, or "do things by the book." And because responsibility is culturally endorsed as a positive virtue, they may fail to realize that being obsessed with it is actually quite unhealthy for them. An overactive Te can contribute to an air of smugness and self-righteousness in ESFPs, detracting from their better virtues of openness (Se) and compassion (Fi).

ESFPs' Inferior Function: Introverted Intuition (Ni)

As is true of other types, ESFPs can be easily blinded to the degree to which their inferior function impacts their decisions and behavior. Without sufficient awareness and integration of their inferior, ESFPs will continue to feel incomplete and be prone to unwise decision-making in their lifestyle, careers, and relationships. ESFPs seeking self-knowledge and personal growth must work to understand the ways their inferior function, Introverted Intuition (Ni), manifests in their personality.

For NJ types, Ni confers a depth of perception and insight. But because Ni is essentially unconscious and undeveloped in ESFPs, they do not enjoy the same degree of access or benefit from its workings. Nonetheless, for reasons I have described elsewhere, their inferior Ni remains highly attractive and alluring. For this reason, ESFPs often delude themselves into believing they are deeply insightful and entitled to function as sages or counselors.

While ESFPs' auxiliary Fi does confer a healthy and genuine concern for friends and loved ones, this differs from the ego boost they receive from using their Ni and Te to proffer advice. In many ways, ESFPs can be understood as trying to validate their self-worth or achieve wholeness through counseling others. And while some ESFPs can seem impressive and convincing in doing so (especially at first blush), like other types, they are prone to overestimating their inferior's capacities. The fact is that, as Se types, they are not wired to function as idea generators or advice givers. When ESFPs fancy themselves as Ni sages, they are being deceived, even if unknowingly, by their ego.

Similar to the Enneagram Two, as described by Riso and Hudson, ESFPs in the grip of their inferior Ni are prideful and self-righteous. They can be slow to see or admit their own personal failures or shortcomings, since this would threaten their self-image of being wise (Ni) and righteous (Te).

Their inferior Ni can also cause ESFPs to latch onto a particular theory, worldview, or plan for their lives. So instead of going with the flow and allowing life to come to them (Se), they try to control life (Te) to ensure it conforms to their Ni vision or ideals. This of course goes against their natural (and healthy) mode of functioning as ESPs. By going against the "natural order" for their type, they are susceptible to unwise decision-making in their careers and relationships.

Healthy functioning for ESFPs, as well as other personality types, involves the development and regular employment of their dominant and auxiliary functions. In truth, ESFPs best insights and decisions come from a breadth of lived experience (Se) and a compassionate outlook (Fi) rather than from indulging their Ni. Understanding this alone is a critical first step for ESFPs seeking enduring peace, wholeness, and life satisfaction.

ESTP

ESTP is the last (but not the least) of our 16 personality types. While some estimates suggest ESTPs comprise only 4% of the general population, my research and experience suggests that estimates of 7% (or higher) are likely to be closer to the mark. ESTP males are thought to outnumber females at a clip of two to one.

ESTPs are fun, active, and charming. Because ESTPs' Thinking function is introverted in its direction (Ti), it often goes unnoticed by outsiders. What others tend to see is ESTPs engaging in action (Se) or with people (Fe). Their tertiary function, Extraverted Feeling (Fe), contributes ample affability and personableness to their outward presentation.

ESTPs typically display conventional, even stylish, forms of dress. While their Ti is concerned with functionality and practicality, their Extraverted Sensing (Se) and Fe functions are attuned to the trendy and popular; social status is often a high priority for ESTPs.

Since their dominant function (Se) is a Perceiving function, ESTPs are naturally more concerned with experiencing the world than they are with structuring or controlling it. And as Extraverts, the outside world serves as their primary source of stimulation. This makes ESTPs the most action-oriented and task-oriented of all types. Without a task or something novel to experience, they can quickly become bored and restless. With adequate stimulation, ESTPs act and respond quickly, making things happen and getting things accomplished. They are "doers," men and women of action.

Like ISTPs, ESTPs display great kinesthetic intelligence. They are athletic and mechanically-inclined, endowed with ample dexterity and hand-eye coordination. In contrast to ENTPs, who exhibit a preponderance of mental energy, ESTPs exhibit great physical energy. ENTPs use Ne to explore new ideas or hypotheticals. ESTPs employ their bodies and senses to explore and manipulate the physical world (Se). Therefore, ESTPs commonly pursue careers that allow them to explore sensory novelties and use their practical intelligence to solve concrete problems (i.e., Holland "Realistic careers). They make excellent chefs, athletes, chiropractors, physical therapists, surgeons, etc. They can also make great performers. Their sense of style and presentation, combined with their kinesthetic capacities, allow them to excel as actors, musicians, and the like.

Because of their preference for hands-on activities, ESTPs may underperform in academic settings. This may not be due to a lack of ability *per se*, but to a lack of Se stimulation. As is true for all SPs, the most concrete of all the personality types, being forced to deal in abstractions for too long can be draining for ESTPs. Their impatience with abstractions may also explain why they are more apt to be diagnosed with ADD or ADHD than some of the other personality types.

ESTPs are generally open and adaptable to new experiences. Despite their status as Extraverts, they often prefer "doing" more than talking. While they may be chatty at times, neither Se nor Ti is a highly verbal function. Thus, ESTPs first instinct is to express themselves via action rather than words. Their relationships are generally built around a breadth of shared activities (Se) rather than extensive, in-depth conversations. But since status and reputation are important to both their Se and Fe, ESTPs may be far more talkative at work or in public settings. In the public arena, they may quickly shift into "schmoozing mode." This can differ dramatically from their private persona, where they can seem more independent and aloof. The ostensible disparity between their public and private personas may at times lead their intimates to consider them narcissistic or hypocritical.

As we've seen, ESTPs' public actions are driven by a need to be admired and respected. This stems, in large part, from their tertiary Fe, which combined with their Se concern for appearances, prompts them to take their social obligations quite seriously. Since their public actions affect their reputation, ESTPs are careful not to act in ways that could jeopardize their social standing. In attempting to maintain a strong public image, they may be particular about punctuality, dressing appropriately, and behaving according to social expectations. This image-consciousness contributes to their tendency to score high as Enneagram Threes.

ESTPs' public conscientiousness may lead them to mistype themselves as ESTJs. But ESTJs, whose dominant function is Extraverted Thinking (Te), tend to be far more blunt and unapologetic in their assertions than ESTPs. ESTPs exude an affability and personableness that is clearly distinguishable from the take-charge, "to-the-point" persona of ESTJs. In social settings, ESTPs can blend and engage with people far more effortlessly than is typical of ESTJs. While ESTPs put people at ease, ESTJs are often uncomfortably direct or opinionated.

Like other Perceivers, ESTPs can have a propensity for acting passively or passive-aggressively in their relationships. Because their Ti precedes their extraverted Fe in their functional stack, ESTPs are more apt to internalize (Ti) or act on (Se) their frustrations than openly talk about them (Fe). This can be frustrating for partners who would prefer to dialogue about their concerns rather than ESTPs taking matters into their own hands. This can be complicated by the fact that, because of their tertiary Fe, ESTPs may prefer to avoid conflict and function, to some degree, as people-pleasers. Hence, ESTPs can find themselves caught between wanting to please their partner, on the one hand, and wanting to convey their frustrations, on the other. This can lead to a situation in which ESTPs are being outwardly compliant while furtively engaging in duplicitous or passive-aggressive behaviors.

ESTPs' Functional Stack & Personality Type Development

ESTPs' functional stack is composed of the following functions:

Dominant: Extraverted Sensing (Se)

Auxiliary: Introverted Thinking (Ti)

Tertiary: Extraverted Feeling (Fe)

Inferior: Introverted Intuition (Ni)

ESTPs' personality type development can be broadly conceived as consisting of three phases:

Phase I (Childhood)

This phase of development is characterized by the emergence of Extraverted Sensing (Se) as ESTPs' dominant personality function. Phase I ESTPs are fun-loving and free-spirited. They enjoy being active and drinking in all the experiences life has to offer. Since their foremost concern is absorbing and experiencing the world, they tend not to take themselves or life itself too seriously. Phase I ESTPs may also show some degree of development in their auxiliary function, Introverted Thinking (Ti).

Phase II (Adolescence-30s)

While the inferior function is not entirely dormant or inert in Phase I, the tug-of-war between the dominant and inferior does not come to the fore until Phase II. Once ESTPs' dominant Se reaches a certain threshold of strength and dominance, their inferior function, Introverted Intuition (Ni), begins to assert itself and play a more significant and mischievous role. This will be elaborated later in this profile. Phase II ESTPs also show increasing use and development of their auxiliary Ti, and may even begin to tap into their tertiary function, Extraverted Feeling (Fe).

Phase III (30s, 40s, & Beyond)

If all goes well and they are fortunate enough to enter Phase III, ESTPs become increasingly aware of the insidious ways of their inferior Ni. As they become more aware of their inferior and learn to function more authentically as ESTPs, they experience greater balance between their Se and Ni. They learn that integrating their Ni happens naturally and indirectly as they go about authentically using their Se and Ti. As they cultivate conditions that support their natural strengths, Phase III ESTPs come to experience a heightened sense of peace, wholeness, and satisfaction.

ESTPs' Dominant Function: Extraverted Sensing (Se)

There are two varieties of Sensing: Introverted Sensing (Si) and Extraverted Sensing (Se). While Si is conservative with respect to the material world, Se is more liberal and novelty-oriented. Se involves the perception of information through the five senses (i.e., sight, smell, touch, sound, and taste). It is sensual, instinctual, and appetitive. Se types love novel sensations, physical thrills, and material comforts. They are "sensation-seekers," relishing novel experiences and the thrill of action.

Se attunes to the concrete details and sensory data of the present by way of the five senses. ESTPs naturally scan the environment for interesting sensory novelties, noticing details that other types might miss.

As a child, I would occasionally go on long car rides with my ESTP father. He loved driving because it provided him with the constant change in scenery needed to stimulate his Se. It was a rare occasion that he failed to "spot" something to bring to my attention: a deer prancing through a distant field, a rare sports car, or a hawk scoping out its prey from above. Only occasionally could he be found directly attending to the road ahead, since he was always on scanning for something novel and interesting.

ESTPs commonly enjoy hobbies that capitalize on their keen powers of observation. My father has always enjoyed keeping his cars in immaculate condition, washing them by hand twice a week. The notion of "detailing" a vehicle aptly describes a primary purpose of Se, involving close attention to the details of the immediate environment.

Se also contributes to ESTPs' love of sports, food, sex, and physical action. As we've seen, ESTPs love working with their hands and quickly responding to environmental demands.

ESTP's Auxiliary Function: Introverted Thinking (Ti)

As dominant Perceivers, ESTPs are naturally disposed to taking a less intentional approach to life. Like other EPs, they are content to remain in an open mode of Perceiving until life demands a response or judgment. When ESTPs are compelled to make judgments a la their auxiliary Ti, they become more inwardly focused and intense, similar to the typical mode of operation for ISTPs. But because Ti is introverted in its direction, onlookers may fail to notice this more serious side of the ESTP.

Ti involves the application of logic and reason for the sake of understanding a given situation, system, or problem. Ti also works to bring structure and order to the inner world. This inner structuring grants ESTPs a good sense of inner control. Inwardly, ESTPs are self-disciplined, working to independently manage their thoughts and objectives.

Ti might also be viewed in terms of *fluid intelligence*, whereas Extraverted Thinking (Te) seems more related to *crystallized intelligence* . Ti is more intuitive, contextual, and right-brained, whereas Te is more abstract, procedure-oriented, and left-brained. The fluid nature of their Ti, combined with the keen observational powers of their Se, contributes to ESTPs' acumen as practical problem solvers. ESTPs can analyze a situation, diagnose the problem, and then determine how to fix it.

The difference between Ti in ESTPs versus ISTPs is its place in the functional stack. For ISTPs, Ti comes first, which makes them characteristically more serious, focused, and quicker to judge. ISTPs then use their auxiliary Se to open up and further explore their initial judgments. For ESTPs, the order is reversed. They do not start with an initial judgment or presumption like ISTPs, but approach things through the open eyes of their Se. They then employ their Ti to evaluate, structure, and order their Se observations. Their Se dominance also makes ESTPs more open to "playing" or perceiving for its own sake.

ESTPs' Tertiary Function: Extraverted Feeling (Fe)

ESTPs' tertiary function is Extraverted Feeling (Fe). Fe is the most interpersonal of all the functions. It strives to promote interpersonal peace, harmony, and understanding. This involves attending not only to *what* is said, but also *how* it is said. It allows ESTPs to quickly establish rapport and connections with others.

Fe also involves a desire to be socially understood and validated. Although ESTPs may not connect with others on a deep level of feeling, their Fe still desires the sense of affirmation and validation that comes from engaging with people. So even though they are Thinking types,

ESTPs need a certain degree of social engagement. As we've seen, they particularly enjoy engaging with others in the public arena.

We can also approach ESTPs' Fe more theoretically. Namely, since Fe serves as their extraverted Judging function and falls lower in their functional stack, they are generally less comfortable extroverting judgments (Fe) than they are keeping their judgments to themselves (Ti). This can lead ESTPs to habitually defer to others' wishes rather than asserting their own, functioning to some extent as "people-pleasers." But because ESTPs have fairly independent minds (Ti), they may eventually grow resentful of others who they may see as trying to control them. This can result in ESTPs functioning unhealthily in what is sometimes described as a "co-dependent" fashion. On the one hand, they feel reliant on their partners for Fe support, while on the other, they feel the need to be unfettered (Se) and independent (Ti).

ESTPs' Inferior Function: Introverted Intuition (Ni)

As is true of other types, ESTPs can be easily blinded to the degree to which their inferior function impacts their decisions and behavior. Without sufficient awareness and integration of their inferior, ESTPs will continue to feel incomplete and be prone to unwise decision-making in their lifestyle, careers, and relationships. Consequently, ESTPs seeking self-knowledge and personal growth must work to understand the ways their inferior function, Introverted Intuition (Ni), manifests in their personality.

ESTPs' inferior Ni may manifest as a desire to be seen as profound or insightful with respect to abstract topics, such as politics or religion. So by asserting and defending certain dogmas or ideologies, ESTPs can experience a strong, even if unhealthy, sense of ego validation.

Since Ni is a fairly convergent function, it may inspire ESTPs to latch onto a single theory, worldview, or plan for their lives. So instead of going with the flow and allowing life to come to them (Se), they may try to force-fit life into a preformed Ni plan. This of course goes against their most natural (and healthy) mode of Se functioning, making them susceptible to unwise decision-making in their careers, relationships, and otherwise.

Healthy functioning for ESTPs, as well as other personality types, involves the development and regular employment of their dominant and auxiliary functions. ESTPs must realize that their best insights and decisions will not come from their immature Ni, but will emerge primarily from gaining a breadth of experiences (Se), combined with rational analyses of those experiences (Ti). When ESTPs extend much beyond their own experiences, they are prone to much greater error and are more likely to fall into the grip of their Ni ego.

BIBLIOGRAPHY

Csikszentmihaly, M. *Flow: The Psychology of Optimal Experience.* Harper. 2008.

Drenth, A.J. *My True Type: Clarifying Your Personality Type, Preferences & Functions.* Inquire Books. 2014.

Drenth, A.J. *The INTP: Personality, Careers, Relationships, & the Quest for Truth and Meaning.* Inquire Books. 2013.

Jung, C.G. *Psychological Types.* Princeton University Press. 1971.

Keirsey, D. *Please Understand Me II.* Prometheus. 1998.

King, T. *Jung's Four and Some Philosophers: A Paradigm for Philosophy.* University of Notre Dame Press. 1999.

Myers, IB, et al. *MBTI Manual: A Guide to the Development and Use of the Myers-Briggs Type Indicator.* 1998.

Thomson, L. *Personality Type: An Owner's Manual. Shambhala.* 1998.

Quenk, N. *Beside Ourselves: Our Hidden Personalities in Everyday Life.* Consulting Psychologists Press. 1993.

ADDITIONAL RESOURCES

To learn more about the 16 personality types, including their careers, relationships, and type development, I encourage you to visit us at:

PersonalityJunkie.com

You may also wish to explore my other books:

My True Type: Clarifying Your Personality Type, Preferences & Functions

The INTP: Personality, Careers, Relationships, & the Quest for Truth and Meaning.

The INTP Quest: INTPs' Search for their Core Self, Purpose, & Philosophy

*If you appreciated this book and would like to promote our work, we always appreciate positive Amazon or iTunes reviews!

81778680R00137

Made in the USA
Middletown, DE
27 July 2018